A BAGFUL OF MONKEYS

George M. Evans

Published with the financial support
of the Welsh Books Council

ISBN: 0-86381-891-9

Cover design: Sian Parri

First published in 2004 by the author;
printed by Gwasg Carreg Gwalch,
12 Iard yr Orsaf, Llanrwst, Wales LL26 0EH
☎ 01492 642031   ▤ 01492 641502
⌂ books@carreg-gwalch.co.uk   Website: www.carreg-gwalch.co.uk

Acknowledgements

I would like to offer my thanks to the following:

My grandchildren Luke, Lisa, Jordan and Larah who inspired me to write this book.

In memory of my father who guided me throughout my boxing career.

Myrddin ap Dafydd, for taking the chance to gamble on publishing my work.

The Arts Council of Wales and the Welsh Book Council without whom it would not have been possible.

My nephew, Barrister, Simon Smith for taking the trouble to read my book and also suggesting the title.

My pal, Paul Boyce with whom I have kept in touch.

Caroline Jacob of Merthyr library for lending me photographs of Merthyr Tydfil.

Foreword

Early Sunday morning in the South Wales valley town of Merthyr Tydfil, men, women and children slowly make their way up the mountainside to an area of open ground where they gather as spectators. The sun is shining, but there is a chill wind that makes two men shudder as they strip to the waist in preparation for combat. There is no fist protection and fighters regularly dip their hands in brine to make the skin as tough as old leather and to protect and harden knuckles. They also wash their faces in brine, but eventually the skin becomes so brittle it splits with every blow landed. Mountain fighters are instantly recognised by the trademarks of broken nose, cauliflower ears, missing teeth, sagging eyebrows and facial scarring. They eat raw meat and drink blood from a slain animal in the belief that it will give them strength.

On the grassy mountain slope, spectators form a circle inside which the fighters will combat. The referee (who is also the promoter and manager of the pugilists) calls the two fighters to the centre of the ring and shouts, 'Are you ready?' On seeing the fighters nod the referee shouts, 'Start,' and they tear into each other. The crowd cheers and waves arms to encourage the fighter they've put money on.

When a man is knocked down it will signal the end of the round and his trainer will run into the ring and assist the fallen fighter to the edge of the circle where he will be revived. Then, once again the ref will call, 'Are you ready?' and the two fighters resume battle.

After numerous facial blows there are several cuts spilling blood. Eventually, one man will be knocked down and fail to rise off the floor. The fighter standing is declared the winner.

Money changes hands among the gamblers and the crowd disperses leaving the battered fighters, their trainers and the promoter standing alone on the mountainside. The fighters then pee on their hands and rub it into their facial cuts in the belief that their urine has healing power. The promoter hands money to the fighters (usually enough for a couple of pints of ale) and they all head for the nearest pub.

During the nineteenth century, the industrial boom in the South Wales valleys enabled steel works and coalmines to increase their trade world wide and there was a demand for labour. Prosperity reigned. Vast numbers of immigrants seeking work were attracted to the area and large communities of various nationalities congregated in Merthyr. But the mixing of different nationalities, religions and cultures often caused friction which resulted in quarrels and fights.

Then, the Depression arrived in the Welsh valleys and the families who had flocked to Merthyr with the promise of work, as well as their South Walian neighbours, suddenly found themselves unemployed, homeless and poor. People wandered the streets looking for non-existent work. Only unemployment was certain.

Many industrialists took advantage of over-manning by reducing wages, causing strife and hardship for those still employed. Hunger marches were organised and the situation became so bad that politicians proposed the complete evacuation of the population of Merthyr to either Usk or the Glamorgan coast. St Tydfil's workhouse which was situated in the centre of Merthyr, and also housed an 'idiot' ward became full to capacity. Malnutrition was rife and cemeteries full. It was at this time that King Edward VIII chose to visit Merthyr and seeing the impoverished community spoke the immortal words, 'Something must be done'.

Many who found themselves without work drifted around the country begging and thieving. Fighting to survive became a way of life. Others would congregate among their own to find shelter and support, forming areas like the infamous China in Merthyr where thieves, prostitutes, murderers and people of the lowest kind gathered. Some would start their own business, roaming the countryside with a grindstone offering to sharpen knives and scissors for a few pence. Others would sing in pubs, happy that their bellies were full even if only with beer. There were some men who would allow their daughters to visit mine owners for an hour or so; did it matter so long as they came home with a side of beef and a few shillings?

Then there were the men who turned to boxing to make a living. Most publicans offered a spare room in their pubs for use as a boxing gym, where boxers training would attract an audience of men who would also quench their thirst with beer. The better known the boxers who could be persuaded to train at the pub then the more customers were attracted and the more beer sold.

Fighting in the industrial valleys was commonplace. Inadequate safety measures at workplaces caused accidents and men who regularly witnessed death and injury became hardened. Church elders were appalled at the way young children idolised mountain fighters and praised the latest winner who was a hero only until he was beaten.

One of the most famous Welsh mountain fighters was Redmond Coleman, who lived in that area of Merthyr called China. Coleman was a strong fighter who, on hearing the shout of 'Start' would wade into his opponent slugging and clubbing until the man dropped.

Apart from mountain fighting, a row between two men in a pub would see them step outside to settle the argument. Other drinkers would follow and form a circle while the two quarrellers stripped to the half, and just like their heroes on the mountainside, start fighting with bare fists.

As time progressed, smarter types could see an 'earner' and the boxing booth, a roped square hanging from four corner posts was introduced. Boxing booths were usually connected to travelling fairs which wandered from town to town and engaged the better fighters who would then take on all comers from the watching crowd. The show attracted mountain fighters wanting to earn money, but few were willing to challenge these fighters who were regarded as being too vicious. Boxers who accepted regular work at boxing booths enjoyed the money earned as well as the experience gained. Becoming known could mean progressing to small hall boxing.

With the increase in boxing, more gyms started to spring up in towns and cities signalling the end of the bare-fisted, beer-drinking street fighters. Fit men fought harder and faster and so, eventually, the number of rounds had to be reduced to compensate. Boxers became trained athletes, very different from their predecessors who managed to fight twenty-five rounds without undertaking intense training.

The boxing manager was born when men started fo fight each other for pay. He offered the fighter a chance to train while he attended to the business side of boxing. A gentleman's agreement would be obtained (handshake and trust), and the partnership would progress. But the poaching of fighters necessitated the signing of a written contract. Since many boxers were semi-literate or not used to the complex issues of written agreements, boxing contracts invariably favoured the manager. At the majority of boxing shows, basic rules were observed, but different promotions had different rules and different weight limits, and rules were often made up as the fight progressed.

Early records are somewhat inaccurate and confusing with many fights being shown as 'no-decision' contests, which means that neither fighter had been knocked out. If a champion took part in a 'no-decision' contest that went the distance he would claim himself the winner, and to have successfully defended his title.

Britain was the first country to tidy up the image of boxing, and the most important change in the history of boxing was in 1865 when the 8th Marquess of Queensberry along with his friend, Llanelli-born John Graham Chambers, a former lightweight champion of Cambridge University devised his famous boxing rules. John Sholto Douglas, the eighth Marquess of Queensberry was asked to put his name to the rules which were also accepted in America.

At the turn of the century, boxing become a major sport which flourished in large industrial areas. Men were rough and tough and their limbs and joints were supple through hard work. Since public transport was inadequate the men walked to their destinations keeping limbs flexible. However, poor quality of life and lack of medical knowledge, as well as environmental pollution resulted in ill health, with the average life expectancy in the Welsh valleys being about forty years. By the end of the nineteenth century prize fighting (bare-fist fighting) had virtually disappeared. The last bare knuckle world heavyweight fight was between John L. Sullivan and Jake Kilrain, both from America in 1889.

The Amateur Boxing Association (ABA) was formed in 1881 and held its first championships in the same year. The first governing body of British boxing was the National Sporting Club, formed in 1891 at 43, King Street, Covent Garden, London, revitalising the Queensberry rules and bringing order to the noble art. In 1909, National Sporting Club President, Lord Lonsdale donated a Challenge Belt that read 'National Sporting Club Challenge Belt', to be presented to winners of the, 'All England Championship', and at the same time weight limits were standardised.

In 1929 the British Boxing Board of Control was formed and took control. It issued licences, promoted the use of regulated boxing gloves as well as rules for contests and medical supervision for boxers. But, because the British Boxing Board conducted a medical for each boxer before a contest the number of those participating in controlled boxing declined. Later, when boxing became socially acceptable, the number of licenced boxers once again increased.

The National Sporting Club Challenge Belt was renamed the Lonsdale Challenge Belt after its donator Lord Lonsdale and the

All England Championship was replaced by the British Championship. If a boxer won the belt three times it was his to keep along with a pension of one pound a week from the age of fifty.

The first Welshman to win a British championship (called the 'All England' title) in 1906 and again in 1909, the year of the inauguration of the Lonsdale belt, was middleweight Tom Thomas from Penygraig in the Rhondda. Tom's contest did not take place at the National Sporting Club but in Pontypridd. For a boxer to achieve a notch on a Lonsdale belt in those days the title contest had to take place under the auspices of the National Sporting Club, which virtually ruled boxing at that time. The first Welsh boxer ever to receive a Lonsdale belt was Pontypridd lightweight Freddie Welsh, when he won the British title in November 1909. The first boxer to win a Lonsdale belt outright by winning it the required three times was featherweight Gentleman Jim Driscoll, of Cardiff, in 1911.

Chapter 1

The past revisited

Determined to revisit one of my previous haunts I journeyed to the city of London, destination the Café Royale on Piccadilly, home to the National Sporting Club where professional boxing shows were held. On reaching the building on Regent Street, I passed beneath the outside canopy, entered the lobby unnoticed by the receptionists who were talking among themselves, and walked to one of the lifts. I stepped inside the lift and asked the attendant for the fourth floor. 'Fourth floor, sir,' he said and closed the door before pressing the required button. There was a slow hum as the lift ascended, then stopped. 'Fourth floor,' repeated the attendant and opened the door.

I stepped out of the lift onto the landing and walked into the elegantly decorated hall with its many dining tables, where only the previous night a professional boxing event had been held.
In the room centre I could see a boxing ring where the boxers had displayed their skills. An array of electric lighting hung suspended from the ceiling. There was the sight of last night's litter covering the floor and chairs left scattered untidily by people eager to leave at the finish.

Feeling the adrenaline start to run through my body I made my way to the ladies' cloakrooms with the plush carpet and décor that were familiar to me. Boxing at the NSC was for men only and on those occasions, the ladies cloakrooms were used as boxers' dressing rooms. From the six chairs lining a wall I took one to a corner and sat alone, where, as a young man, I had prepared myself for engagement in the hardest profession.

My fingers automatically rubbed my swollen eyebrows, streaked with scar tissue as a result of cutting badly during fights, and my knuckles where a doctor had injected a painkiller before each fight. I looked around the room and my gaze came to rest on a pair of blood and grease stained boxing gloves hanging from a nail on one of the walls. The gloves when new would have been bright crimson in colour with white laces, but after years of battering they had become misshapen and the laces stained a dirty grey. I stared at the boxing gloves that took me back in time and suddenly the changing room came to life.

At one end of the room full of people who appeared to be busy but doing nothing, a young fighter, good looking with dark features, weighing about ten stone, was changing into boxing gear of smart yellow silk trunks with a black strip down the side. He wore black leather boots from the tops of which protruded white socks and he was ready to take part in the evening's action. His middle-aged, track-suited trainer, who was short and stocky with an untidy head of grey hair, cut strips of plaster into short lengths and stuck them on the wall.

The fighter's manager, in his thirties, tall and thin in stature with black hair combed back was smartly dressed in a light grey three piece suit and stood watching as the trainer pulled an empty chair in front of the boxer and said, 'Right, let's see then.' The boxer sat astride the chair and put his hands over the back while the trainer bandaged them. Then the trainer took the strips of plaster off the wall and laid them in lengths over the back of the boxer's bandaged hands and around his knuckles, until each fist was as solid as a club.

'How'd you feel?' asked the trainer as he held up the palm of his hand for the boxer to punch. The boy let go with his fists and

I could hear 'smack, smack!' as they connected with the trainer's palm.

'Feels good,' said the boxer and sat back on the chair.

The manager took the six-ounce gloves off the nail, handed one to the trainer and they both started putting them on the boxer's taped hands.

Dress-suit clad Freddie, the whip, looked worried. Desperate to start the show on time he rushed from one dressing room to another checking on the fighters. The door opened and Freddie's head appeared. 'Are you ready?' he asked. Seeing a nod the head disappeared again and the nervous boxer jumped to his feet and started shadow boxing around the room. The manager put a towel around his fighter's shoulders and they left the dressing room on the journey into the arena.

Dinner suited patrons would have finished eating their meal before the boxing started. Many would also have been conducting business over their wine.

I could hear the boxers being announced then the sound of a bell to start the first round and the cheering between rounds. At the National Sporting Club, clapping and cheering during the contest is forbidden. There was loud applause as the contest ended and I could hear cheering when the winner was announced.

Shortly afterwards, the boxer, whose eyebrow had been cut, entered the dressing room with his handlers and flopped, exhausted onto a chair.

'You should have had the decision,' said the manager, who was obviously annoyed.

The fighter said nothing, just stared at the floor.

'I'm going to complain to the Board,' the manager continued.

'That's right,' chipped in the trainer. 'I thought it was a bloody liberty.'

'Quick, watch the door,' said the manager as he held the boxer's head back and looked at the cut over his eye. To stop the cut bleeding during the contest, the manager, instead of using the required adrenaline to block the torn arteries, had put a chewing gum like substance into the wound that hardened like steel when exposed to air. It required the use of small tweezers to remove the banned substance from the wound before the doctor arrived.

Just as the manager finished, the doctor entered. He looked closely at the cut over the eyebrow, shook his head and muttered something before proceeding to wipe blood away. Then he stitched the skin together, sprayed white powder onto the closed wound and asked the fighter if he was all right before hurrying back into the hall to watch the other fights.

The NSC matchmaker, who was short, vastly overweight and dressed in a dinner suit entered the dressing room, smoothed back his grey hair and put his hand on the fighter's shoulder. 'I thought you should have had a draw at least Johnny.'

He turned to the young manager, led him to a corner of the room where they were alone and asked, 'What's your fighter doing in two weeks?'

The manager shook his head. 'He had a hard fight tonight Les and needs a rest.'

'Need time off, what for? He boxed well didn't he and should have had the verdict?'

'I know that Les, but he still had a hard fight.'

The matchmaker continued. 'Is he married then?'

The manager nodded.

'Ave he got any kids?'

The manager nodded again.

'Well, there you are then, he probably needs the money.'

The manager knew the matchmaker was trying to corner him.

'Who do you want to match him with, and what about the cut over his eye?'

'Now I didn't say anything about an opponent did I, just asked if he was willing to fight. The cut's not deep and will heal well enough in two weeks. Go and see how he feels about it. I'll give him an extra hundred quid.'

'Who d'you want him to fight?' The manager was getting flustered now and beginning to sweat. The last thing he wanted was to have a row with the matchmaker of the NSC where there were regular boxing shows.

'A return with the boy who beat him tonight,' said the matchmaker. 'He should have had the decision. Now's his chance to put it right.'

The manager returned to his fighter and said, 'You've been offered a return in a fortnight against the same fella who beat you tonight, and he's offered a hundred pounds extra.'

The fighter looked at his manager, 'Sure I'll take it, I'll beat him next time.'

The manager went in search of the matchmaker although he wasn't happy about the return in two weeks. He'd been coerced into taking the fight, maybe after a longer layoff?

There again, the fight had been close, perhaps it would go the other way next time.

I came back to the present and was alone once more in the dressing room. I smiled and looked around until my gaze returned to the boxing gloves.

After a while the dressing room came to life again and there was excitement and tension in the air because a British Champion was defending his newly won title at the National Sporting Club. The featherweight champion sat in a chair waiting for his manager to wrap his hands in tape and bandage given by a Boxing Board official. Boxers taking part in championship contests must use hand dressings provided by the BBBC, while an official watches the fighters' hands being bandaged, then inspects and puts an official stamp on them when complete. Only brand new boxing gloves are used.

The dressing room was busy. There were newspaper reporters, managers, trainers, ex-fighters, officials and half a dozen hangers on wanting to be around the champion. The champ tried to relax. This fight was important to him and his family. Apart from the money, this was his first defence of the title and winning would give him two notches on the Lonsdale Belt. A third would entitle him to keep it along with a small pension from the age of fifty.

The referee who was officiating the title fight entered the dressing room and talked to the champion about how the rules of boxing must be adhered to. The whip entered the dressing room and said, 'They're waiting,' and walked back out.

It was time to leave for the arena and as they walked toward the hall people were shouting, 'Good luck boyo, give him one for me.'

There was a short wait, then a voice boomed over the microphone. 'Order please,' and all went quiet.

I could hear both fighters being introduced and applauded, and for the next hour or so I could hear the oos and aahs, the thumping of feet on canvas and the ringing of the timekeeper's bell. Then the bell rang to end the last round of the contest and there was a tremendous roar as the ref raised the winner's arm. I was anxious, wondering who had won the fight.

The door of the dressing room opened and the smiling champion entered along with a crowd of happy people. The champion had successfully defended his title. Within minutes the dressing room was full. The doctor arrived to check the fighter is okay; newspaper reporters crowd in along with the matchmaker, a promoter, and men crowding around the fighter saying, 'We did it, How', we did it'. I failed to see how the plural could be used when only the fighter had blood coming from his mouth and one eye closed. Friends and family the champion didn't know he had appeared, all wanting to be in on the act.

'Yea,' one bloke said, 'the Champ and I are pals from way back.' The champ was in a happy mood and agreed even though he had never met the guy before.

It was a long time before business had been conducted, well-wishers had gone and the happy entourage left.

Once more, I was back to the present and staring at the boxing gloves on the wall. I willingly allowed myself to drift back in time and the dressing room became busy again.

While a boxer was changing, his manager, short of build and greasy faced, took the boxing gloves off the wall, put his hand in one and started to punch the wall with the intention of flattening the filling on the knuckle part. The same process was repeated with the other glove and then he put them back onto the nail. The manager then started taping the fighter's hands, only this time the bandage and tape were illegally put over the knuckles as well. A roll of masking tape was produced and wrapped around the fighter's knuckles before being covered with more tape to hide the cheating. There was no official inspection as this was only required for championship bouts. The proverbial head appeared and shouted, 'Ten minutes,' and the manager and fighter grinned at each other and left the room. Some time later they return to the dressing room. The fighter was obviously victorious and not guilty about how he won.

I was still in a dream when I recognised another fighter who appeared in the doorway and looked around before entering. He was thirty-year-old Len Morgan who walked to one of the chairs and sat down, slinging his bag of gear onto the floor and yawning. After years in the fight game he had the tell tale marks of sagging eyebrows, ears like bits of warped gristle and a nose that was much wider than it should have been.

I instantly recognised his situation. He was at the end of his boxing career, hadn't trained properly and taken the fight at a moment's notice. He'd spent the afternoon travelling to arrive in time to box. Len Morgan's manager had long ago started making excuses not to travel with him, but would still expect his 25% fee. Len would have to look after his own affairs this evening. He had been advised to retire after a long boxing career, but was still offered lots of fights and paid good money. Of course he wouldn't admit that he was being used as fodder for up and coming young boxers who wanted a win. He was now what they called a journeyman.

Len put his head back and looked at the ceiling, probably thinking, 'Was it all worth it?' He'd earned money during his professional career but where had it all gone? Yes, he'd made up his mind, this was going to be his last contest. It would be a hard fight tonight that he didn't really want to take, but the matchmaker had asked him to do it as a favour, recalling all the good times they'd had, all the fights he'd been given at the Sporting Club, until Len felt guilty and obliged. The dressing room began to fill up and everybody acknowledged the fighter by his first name.

Len started to change. There would be the doctor to see but no need to weigh-in; the matchmaker had said he'd fix it for him. The fighter didn't realise that it was assumed he would lose and that there was no need for his opponent to worry about weight. Having changed and been examined by the doctor, Len stood alone wondering who he could persuade to help him prepare for battle and assist him in the corner. Finally he offered an unknown trainer a tenner to bandage his hands, glove him up and help him in his corner.

It was time to go into the hall and box and, followed by the trainer, Len left the dressing room. I could hear the crowd clap as he and his opponent entered the ring. Once again I could hear the noise of two men fighting and the audience applauding between rounds. Then the fight ended. There was more applause and after a while Len returned to the dressing room. By all accounts there had been a hard fought contest and that was obvious from the way Len's face was battered and bleeding.

'How'd it go son?' someone asked.

The disillusioned fighter shrugged his shoulders. 'Should have won, but there you are, that's the way it goes.'

Len quickly washed and dressed, then looked for the matchmaker to collect his purse money before catching the last train home to Cardiff. No one said, 'Cheerio' or, 'See you again' as they had done when he was younger and winning fights.

I stopped daydreaming and returned to the present where I thought about my introduction into boxing. Good or bad, it was a means to an end and I became a boxing statistic. For seven years I fought for pay and for another twenty conducted business as a boxing trainer, manager and promoter. My home town of Merthyr

Tydfil, for decades known as a boxing town had been the deciding factor in my life. I ventured into boxing because it was a way out of the poverty trap, and the way to a little bit of glory, however small. Whatever the reason, it was what I chose.

Chapter 2

Billy and Maud

It all began with the birth of my father, William (Billy) Theophilus Evans, on 10th February, 1910 in a small, terraced, two bedroomed worker's cottage that lacked basic commodities and bordered the main road of Plymouth Street in the lower part of Merthyr Tydfil, where poverty existed and shoeless children, dressed in rags wandered the roads. The roar of automobiles and charabancs was infrequent, and manure on the main road gave proof to the popularity of horse drawn transport.

The front door of the cottage opened into a small front room which led to a smaller kitchen, whose commodities comprised a cold-water tap over a stone bosh (Merthyr slang for 'sink'), a cast iron fire grate that heated an oven for cooking and oil lamps that provided light. At the front of the cottage stood a small brick lavatory that was flushed with a bucket of water and to the side of which a row of stone steps led to the main road. At the back of the cottage ran a tramline.

My father's mother died while he was four years old and his father, Morgan Evans, reared him and his six year old sister Tydfil, with the help of their 12 year old sister Irene and their 16 year old brother Harry. Morgan Evans, a small, energetic man of confirmed Welsh stock, worked as a masseur for local mine owners, massaging the battered limbs of miners injured underground and making them well enough to go back to work. He also assisted doctors at local hospitals. Morgan was a tough little fellow, who often stripped to the half to fight an opponent bare knuckle outside a public house and on a Sunday morning ran races for money. He was regarded as a local hero for his acts of bravery, which include diving fully clothed into Glyn-Mill Pond to rescue a drowning man. For this he was presented with a silver pocket watch and chain inscribed, 'Presented to Morgan Evans on behalf of the Soldiers Fund' (a charity run mainly to send parcels to solders fighting during WW1), at the Mountain Ash Inn. And for jumping aboard a runaway tram taking miners to work and bringing it to a halt, he was presented with a gold medal inscribed 'Presented to Morgan Evans, for bravery on the 30th June, 1918'.

Like most Merthyr kids of that time Billy had a fairly rough upbringing and as a lad walked bare foot and knew the pains of hunger, as he and others queued at soup kitchens. Throughout the end of the nineteenth century Cholera had killed vast numbers because of a lack of sanitation. Scores of houses were unfit for habitation and the death rate was high. Although Morgan Evans worked regularly, like most working class men, his pay was small and he also frequented public houses.

Fighting was second nature in the valleys. Like many young boys, Billy Evans fought on the street, in amateur boxing shows and boxing booths, learning the trade early in life. Poverty and hunger conditioned people to a streetwise attitude that became an instinct for survival.

With the formation of the Boxing Board of Control in 1929 a boxer required a licence and Billy was granted a boxer's licence on the 11th June, 1933. He fought as a bantamweight. He was a tough, box fighter, with one hell of a punch developed by swinging a sledgehammer as a smithy's striker at the local Gasworks. He would stand in the centre of the boxing ring swaying off his hips thus making himself a difficult target to hit. In those early days of boxing there was little control and many boxers broke the few rules which did exist. On a Saturday afternoon, Billy would box as an amateur at the Welfare, Troedyrhiw, and then in the evening at the Merthyr Labour Club marquee as a 'pro'. Many times Billy and his mates walked over the mountain from Merthyr to Bargoed, fought for a purse of ten shillings and then walked all the way back home to Merthyr.

My mother, Maud Aris, was born to better circumstances on the 9th August, 1919 to Merthyr-born Lilian Maud and George Aris from Surrey, England, who as a young man emigrated to Australia where he trained to be a printer. He worked his way back to Britain on a steamer and settled in the South Wales town of Merthyr where he met and married Lillian Maud. George Aris became manager of the *Merthyr Express* newspaper and at the same time accepted the role of secretary of the near bankrupt Merthyr Labour Club, saving it from closure and making it the most profitable in Merthyr. As 'sec' of the Labour Club George Aris managed variety acts and the then popular concert parties that toured the working men's clubs. He also took advantage of the glut of tough young men who came to Wales by promoting boxing shows in a marquee erected in the grounds of the Labour Club.

But a terrible tragedy was to befall the Aris family. When Maud was just eight years old her mother died, leaving her and older sister Connie to be reared by their father and a Mrs Roderick, taken on as live-in housekeeper. Mrs Roderick moved into the family home with her own two daughters shortly before Lilian Aris died. Maud's grief was twofold when the housekeeper, who became George Aris's lover, took a dislike to the fondness shown to Maud by her father and began treating her coldly at a time when she needed love and comfort most of all.

The day of the funeral arrived and Lilian Maud's coffin was placed in the parlour where family and friends paid their respects. Mrs Roderick admonished Maud for kissing her dead mother. Maud ran upstairs and watched from a front bedroom window as her mother's coffin was carried from the house and put into the first motorised hearse to be used in Clare Street.

With Lilian Aris dead, Mrs Roderick dominated the weak willed George Aris and took control over the household. The housekeeper began to mentally abuse the eight-year-old Maud, making life miserable for the little girl. Maud Aris dearly loved her father who, in his way, loved his young daughter but she longed for more affection. As a teenager, Maud grew into an attractive, blonde young lady who became an accomplished piano accordionist much in demand to play at theatres nationwide.

Professional boxer Billy Evans, managed by George Aris, first met Maud at the Britannica Public House, one of a number of pubs in Plymouth Street that lay at the lower end of Merthyr where George Aris had booked Maud to play the accordion. Billy Evans, a dapper, smartly dressed, good looking young man with black hair had been training at the pub's gym and was noticed by Maud who enquired who he was. George Aris told Maud that he was a boxer, didn't do any studying, wouldn't get anywhere and that she was to have nothing to do with him!

Then the unthinkable happened! Billy, a common fighter, and Maud started courting and fell in love, and met regularly in secret. Maud had at last found the affection she'd been looking for. Billy would love and protect her for the rest of his life. But George Aris found out about the relationship between the fighter and his daughter and arranged for Maud to tour South Africa playing the accordion. His intention was to keep the couple apart in the hope that Maud would forget her new-found love.

The year was 1937 when Billy and Maud discovered the plan to part them and they eloped and married. But this move caused conflict in both families. My father's family thought he'd married above himself and my mother's family thought she had married beneath her station. However, when they arrived back in Merthyr, George Aris forgave his daughter and rented her and her new husband a three bedroomed terraced house that he owned at 11, Clare Street, Merthyr, which they later purchased and it became the family home.

My sister, Marilyn Jane was the first born to Billy and Maud, a bright girl rising to the top in all subjects at school and the first girl from Merthyr to be accepted to London University. From university Marilyn became a doctor, then a consultant psychiatrist. On the 17th February, 1943, I entered the world and like my sister was born during World War Two. The sound of enemy bombers passing overhead must be blamed for startling my mother into dropping me head first down the stairs. Then later, dropping me head first into a bucket before I was one year old. Marilyn and I grew up in a disorientated world of 'in between families,' wondering why Aunts and Uncles ignored us.

Billy, suffering from badly cut eyebrows retired as a boxer and became a boxing trainer, manager and promoter. But he wasn't a businessman and looked after boxers for no financial reward, content with being in the sport he loved. Once, he promoted a boxing show in Brecon, Mid Wales, and after paying rent for the hall, transporting the ring from Merthyr and fighting on the bill himself for nothing, he still lost money. Why did he bother? To know the answer you would have to be like many who have boxing in their blood, and are happy to be involved in the sport just for the pleasure of it.

Chapter 3

Starting School

Finally, that fateful day spoken about by my parents had arrived, the day for me to start school. So young and innocent was I at two and a half years old, being introduced to the outside world and its bullying, bad language, sex and much, much more that became part of growing up. On the morning in question, I washed and dressed in clean clothes before my mother looked at me and announced that it was time to go. A similar instruction is spoken when a condemned man is about to be led to the scaffold! We walked out of our front door and my mother looked across to a house where nearly all the children had died of TB, shook her head and said, 'Poor souls, lovely girls they were.'

That walk from my home in Clare Street to Caedraw, a rundown residential area was full of wonder for me and I was feeling apprehensive. I held my mother's hand as we walked along our street of terraced houses to where the main railway line passed, and across Warlow Street to the main road where the intermittent flow of daily traffic spluttered along. We passed familiar landmarks like the prefabricated hut (known as The Centre), built during World War Two where men and boys idled their time playing darts and snooker; and Billy Porter's paper shop where a gang of boys filled canvas bags with newspapers ready for delivering. We stood aside to let a little man whose legs were seized beneath him pass us. 'Georgie no legs,' sat all day long on a small cart that he propelled along using tiny walking sticks. 'Keep away from the walls so as not to dirty your clothes,' warned Mam.

The majority of households burned coal fires and smoke poured from chimneys leaving a fine dust clinging to everything and entering lungs. Birds were frequently interrupted in their singing to give faint coughs as they cleared the tar-tangled phlegm from their tiny throats. The sound of young babies crying could be heard from upstairs windows as they too tried to clear the collection of coal dust from their chests. When a front door opened the filth entered, curling itself around the inside of houses and clinging to walls, furniture, curtains and Mam's washing that was hanging in front of the fire to air. But the washing had already been discoloured while hanging on the outside line.

Merthyr Council's road cleaners were made up of about half a dozen workmen who walked the roads looking for rubbish they'd shovel into handcarts. Very often the rubbish missed the carts and ended back on the road. The once weekly rubbish collections consisted of a lorry with sliding partitions on the back, left open for the workmen to empty the rubbish bins into. While bins were tipped, clouds of dust ascended, clinging to everything.

On we walked, past a grocery store where Mam was going to buy me an apple, but she realised that she still owed last week's food bill and couldn't 'book' so we carried on walking.

We passed housewives leaning on sweeping brushes while nosing at the goings on, then past a sweet shop, pubs, lodging houses, chapels and garages before reaching Caedraw Junior and Infants school.

On one side of the school that was surrounded by a high, stone wall stood old man Pippins' scrap yard, part of the railway goods yard and the evil smelling river Taff, polluted by poisons poured into it by local industries. The stench of chemicals rose from the river of flowing sewerage. Rats and playing children frequented the banks of what was said to be the fastest rising and falling river in Wales. Lining the rocks and pebbles in the river were old prams, tins, boxes and other rubbish. There was little concern about this and perhaps through ignorance children were allowed to play there, frequently wading into the water to pick up little tin boats thrown from the windows of Triang Toy Factory. On the other side of the school was an area of old houses and pubs called Cross Keys, where the Iron Fountain stood and the foreboding Parish church in the centre of an untidy graveyard.

We walked through large wooden gates into the yard of the old Victorian stone, two-story building, through the main entrance into a large hall where my mother said 'Goodbye' and I was left standing with other kids looking around and wondering. A number of women teachers looked at us with expressionless faces as if to say, 'Oh boy, here we go again'. Other teachers rubbed their knobbly hands together in glee at the thought of being able to, 'Break in another batch of brats.' My first day at school was an experience not to my liking.

The infants' section of Caedraw School was on the ground floor of the building and for a period every afternoon, all children under a certain age were made to lie on a cot or tabletop and told to sleep (what the hell for?). It was strange to me and I wasn't even able to close my eyes. The result was being shouted at by the teacher which made me cry. This was followed by a slap on the top of my leg to, 'Give me something to cry for.'

Teachers took it upon themselves to treat the children exactly as they liked. Parents accepted corporal punishment as being part of school life and having suffered the same themselves they dared not complain and so hid the hurt they felt.

On being forced to lie down, I spent the time looking around the hall with its high, cold, painted walls. (Most of the other kids lying on beds or tabletops were actually sleeping. Bloody hell, didn't they sleep during the night?)

Set into one of the walls was a large iron fire grate that forever lacked the warmth of a coal fire, but we were allowed to keep our coats on sometimes during winter. One winter it was so cold a fire had to be lit, and the teachers continually stood in front of it. Free bottles of milk for pupils were frozen and teachers put them in front of the fire to thaw before doling them out for us to drink. Yuck! There were wooden hoops that were used to support the wall standing in the corner of the main hall. They must have been used for that purpose because none of the kids were ever allowed to move them to play with!

'Right children, time to wake up,' shouted a teacher and I was off the bed like a shot. 'Everyone sit! No talking, no laughing, sit still.' (Is it all right if we breathe, Miss?)

One day every week, all the school children had to line up and drink a spoonful of white liquid poured from a bottle. The teacher, using the same unwashed spoon for all the kids was obviously observing health laws! Little wonder we were regularly off sick. Somebody, somewhere must have heard my pleas because, after about twelve months the nursery section was discontinued (so they told my mother) and I was back at home.

But the time soon went and before I knew it, I was five years old and toeing the line at Caedraw Infants School. 'No peace for the wicked they say.' By this time my sister Marilyn, also at Caedraw School was proving to be a scholar. But I wondered why I was being made to attend school when it was obvious that I didn't want to go there. Fighting and bullying among schoolboys was regular and seemed to be accepted, although why older boys had to thump me I couldn't understand. Attending school was a tough old business and to survive one had to play the game.

Having survived Caerdraw school until seven years of age we were moved upstairs where our new teacher, Miss Davies, a miserable woman took great delight in shouting at the kids.

Now why did she have to keep smacking me on the back of my head? All the desks were together in pairs and I remember that the boy from Caedraw that I sat next to always had green snot hanging from his nose. Just when you thought it was going to drop onto his shirt he'd give a quick sniff dragging it back into his nostrils, where it would start its slow decent all over again.

The headmaster, Mr Hughes, was a short, stocky man with a pleasant face. He'd come into the classroom and say. 'Right oh, I'm taking all you boys to play football.'

'Oh great,' we thought, 'We'll be given football boots and kit supplied by the school.' Not quite! We played in the clothes and shoes we had on! Never mind. By playing football with the school every week, who knows, we may emerge as good professional footballers. No chance! Four years in the Juniors and we were taken to the top of the Donkey tip only about half a dozen times to play football.

I will always remember the headmaster calling the boys together and saying. 'Remember boys, the game you are playing is called soccer not football. Football is rugby, the real name of football is soccer. Now is that quite clear?'

When the bell rang to finish school all the well-behaved kids went straight home, while the rest of us ran over the bridge crossing the river Taff to play among the old workings at Rhydycar, where a number of small cottages nestled below a colliery waste tip. Later in the day, on our home patch in Clare Street, pal Raymond and I would be playing wrestling on the ground as Mrs Thomas walked past. It was a ploy to try and see up her skirt! My mother said that Mrs Thomas wore a fur coat but had no knickers on!

Then, as if by magic, news went around that one of the local girls was under the arches. We'd run as fast as we could until catching sight of the girl would make us draw up. There were two kinds of girls, those that did and those that didn't. She was the first kind. She stood against the wall holding up her skirt while a number of boys queued up, waiting their turn. But alas,

I was only seven and considered too young to take part! Never mind, I'd walk along Plymouth Street instead looking into the gutter for nips thrown there by someone who had finished smoking. Few people smoked tipped cigarettes. Having collected a handful of nips I'd take them to my Bopa's and put tobacco from the nips into one of my grandfather's pipes, light up and have a smoke.

Our valley was partly a mining valley and the miners suffered from the dust disease, pneumoconiosis, which hardened the lungs and prevented air from being pumped into the body. It was normal to see men walking along the pavement coughing, spluttering, bringing up lumps of phlegm from their lungs and then spitting it into the gutter or onto the pavement where people tried not to step in it.

My uncle Harry was one that suffered. As doorman of the Merthyr Labour Club, uncle Harry walked a mile or so from the bottom of town where he lived to the club every night. On occasions, while walking along Plymouth Street I'd hear my name being called and turn to see Uncle Harry leaning against a wall trying to get his breath. He'd motion for me to go to him and I'd have to escort him, stopping every few yards for him to try and get his lungs to pump air into his pain racked body. Uncle Harry struggled to live on the dole and found it hard going with ill health and having to rear my young cousin, Lawrence, on his own.

Lawrence's mother, my aunt Kate, spent her life in the bedroom of their one up, one down cottage, frequently putting her head out of the window and shouting at passers by. Like a lot of working class women in Merthyr, aunt Kate spent most of her married life rearing her children in a tiny terraced house with no facilities other than a cold-water tap. She had to 'make do' on poor money while my uncle Harry spent a lot of his time in the Merthyr Labour club. The pressure told on Aunt Kate. On top of this, she gave birth to my cousin Lawrence during 'the change of life' a woman experiences. Ignorance of the menopause and a lack of understanding for a woman in that situation meant that aunt Kate did not receive sympathy or proper medical attention. The result was that she was taken away to a mental institution where she eventually died.

I was now at an age when I began to take notice of the boxing talk that went on between my father, his friends and my uncles who visited. As they sat in front of the coal fire, the finer points of the noble art would be discussed, as well as who they thought was the best fighter at that time. The local favourite was Merthyr's Eddie Thomas, who on 15th November, 1949 won the British Welterweight Championship by beating Henry Hall on points, and later the European and Commonwealth titles. The frequent talk of boxing and the sight of boxing paraphernalia hanging around our house was normal to me, as was meeting old fighters who regularly visited our home to see my father. It become clear to me that fighting and boxing played a big part in the life of Merthyr Tydfil. It was professional boxers that I looked up to. Policemen and doctors were respected; politicians were respected; teachers and solicitors were respected but they were not admired or idolized. In a young boy's mind it was the fighters who commanded respect and admiration.

The post WW2 period saw a slow improvement in living standards. The government was no longer required to spend on the war effort and looked towards redevelopment throughout the country. During the war the British Government took control over the country's manufacture and production, but only the Government stamp was seen after the War when controls were relaxed and private companies put their own logos on produce. Welsh MP, Aneurin Bevan, introduced the National Health Service and my mother was determined to take advantage of it. She took me to the clinic for anything offered. I was given a pair of National Health spectacles that I never wore and as far as I knew I didn't even have poor eyesight. My visit to the dentist was quite an experience. They didn't bother to give us kids fillings. If you had a bad tooth, out it came!

The time came when I had toothache and my mother made an appointment for me to have the tooth removed. We arrived at the clinic in the centre of Merthyr and sat in the waiting room for what seemed like ages until a door opened. A nurse's head appeared and we were asked to go in to the dentist's room where I could see a big black chair, a table on which were torture instruments and a black rubber mask hanging from a canister. The dentist, who was a big man, looked at me and said, 'Right, get on the chair.' That morning, he must have lost a pound note, judging by the look of thunder on his face. Without warning, the nurse held me tightly in the chair and the dentist forced a rubber mask over my face. I couldn't breath. They were suffocating me. Then I was awake, the ceiling was swaying and I was feeling sick. There was a plastic bib hanging around my neck and the nurse held a tray into which I was spitting blood. 'Right, up you get,' said the dentist and the nurse pulled me, staggering, from the chair. My mother caught hold of me and guided me out of the torture chamber.

Next came the long walk home, holding onto my mother's arm for support and stopping every so often to be sick. But hold on a minute, these were the good old days. What about the other kids? Did they suffer as well? Of course they did, it was the same for us all. The only one with a smile on her face was my mother who obviously thought she'd got something else out of the government.

Chapter 4

A Boxing Boom

The country was beginning to re-establish itself after the war but like other sports, boxing declined, with fighters who had enlisted not returning to the game. Of those who continued to box, Merthyr's Eddie Thomas, became a popular champion. But in June 1951 Eddie lost his European title and in October of the same year he lost his British title.

The famous Guest Keen Dowlais was the last remaining steel works in the Merthyr Valley. A number of mines still produced coal, but where coal mines once thrived, abandoned slag tips now stuck out of the mountainside. An accumulation of factories had sprung up providing low paid work and many families were moved to live in hastily built council prefabricated houses with modern conveniences. Communities were beginning to re-establish themselves and a release from the daily grind for many was watching Merthyr football team play, or to follow the return to boxing of the faded ex Welterweight Champion Eddie Thomas, whose eventual retirement left no active boxers in Merthyr.

After a great pugilistic era, boxing in Merthyr ceased to exist. The war had taken its toll and many public houses closed their doors and with them went the boxing gyms. Few gave thought to the young lads walking the streets with nothing in the way of entertainment and there were no longer amateur boxing clubs where they could be taught boxing. Youngsters could only listen to old men talk about the old days when boxing thrived, referring to George Aris's marquee, Ernie Snow's Pavilion and other boxing shows in the Welsh valleys. Merthyr once famous for producing professional boxers saw the sport fade into obscurity, and fathers subconsciously looked towards their sons to follow the sport they themselves had followed or taken part in. For me it was boxing.

I was eight years old when my father took me to a large, dilapidated building, formerly the Angel Hotel, in Merthyr. The forbidding building was now empty except for the top floor where men trained. My father, in his late thirties, had long since finished boxing but he liked to keep fit and one evening at home I was told, 'Get your training stuff together, George. We're going to the gym.' Mam came into the living room and handed me a pair of dark green silk trunks she had made. The only trunks I'd seen kids wear were hand me downs and I didn't want to be the odd one out so I objected. 'I'm not wearing 'em,' I said. Mam, who'd gone into the kitchen, walked back into the living room. 'Silly boy, you will wear them, tell 'im Bill.' My father came into the room and handed me a brown paper carrier bag. 'You will wear them, put your stuff in there.' My 'stuff' being the silk trunks and a pair of plimsoles (commonly known as 'daps'). There wasn't a sound from my sister, Marilyn, who was sitting in the corner reading. My father, who'd joined my mother in the kitchen shouted, 'George, bring the blacking and your shoes in here for me to polish.' He felt that shoes should always be kept polished.

'I'll polish 'em,' I said and walked to the cupboard where all the polish brushes and dusters were kept.

'Do a good job now,' shouted my father as he went about getting himself ready. I set about with tin of blacking and two brushes, one brush to put the polish on the shoes, the other to vigorously rub and make them shine.

'I'll light the gas 'fore I go,' said Dad, lifting a cushion on the settee and taking an old newspaper he ripped off a piece, screwed it into a quill and took a light from the fire. Then, reaching up to the gas lamp that hung from the centre of the ceiling he pulled one of the little brass chains that released the gas, put the lighted paper to the flow of gas and the room brightened with an eerie, yellowish glow. My father was rushing around making sure he hadn't forgotten anything. 'Come on,' he said and hurried towards the front door.

It was almost dusk out on the street and people stood on their doorsteps watching others walking to and fro, keen to pass the time of day with them.

'Hello Bill, where you going then?' It was Ronnie Thomas, come to have one last look outside before settling in by the fire to listen to the wireless.

'We're going to the gym, Ron,' answered Dad. 'Show him your new trunks George.'

I reached into the carrier bag, pulled out the satin trunks and held them for Ron to look at.

'They're nice George,' he said. 'You'll be posh wearing them.'

But I didn't want to be posh! I put them back in the bag and hoped we wouldn't meet anybody else we knew. We walked up the street and my father started whistling through his teeth. He was always whistling or singing.

''Ello, Mrs Powney.' Dad acknowledged an old lady standing on her doorstep.

''Ello, Mr Evans.'

We walked across to Plymouth Street and I was hopping back and fore from the pavement to the road and back again as we walked. Then on reaching one of the street gas lamps I put my arm around it and swung a couple of times.

'Where you going Will?' It was my Bopa, my father's sister, Tydfil, and she always called my father Will. Bopa had been a widow for many years since my uncle, who I didn't get to meet, died of cancer.

She repeated the question. 'Where you going Will?'

'We're going to the gym,' answered Dad. We didn't stop and I was glad or I'd have had to show Bopa my new trunks.

'Oh aye! That's it,' shouted Bopa at my father as we walked up Plymouth Street. 'Get him knocked about. That's it, you'll learn, you'll learn,' and she carried on walking down the road.

We walked past shops whose doorways smelled of urine from last night's drunks, and where newspapers that had wrapped fish and chips were lying in the gutter thrown there by the same inebriated persons. As we walked beneath the railway bridge a steam engine passed overhead spraying us with grit and I wiped my eyes to clean the muck away. On we walked past the red brick urinal that always smelled of pee, and houses and shop fronts covered with a layer of dust.

I'd stare at the characters always hanging around town like Harry the black, so called because of his colour. Black people were rarely seen in Merthyr and Harry lived in one of the many lodging houses that were dotted about town.

We passed pubs with their smell of stale beer, and garages where the floors were covered with oil and grease. It seemed as if more petrol was tipped onto the floor than put into cars.

Suddenly my Father looked down. 'George what have you done? You naughty boy you've got blacking all over your socks.'

I followed my father's gaze and could see that, in my haste (or perhaps in a daydream), instead of taking my footwear off to polish them I had left them on, missed the shoes and rubbed blacking all over my light grey socks. I could see that my father was angry as he pulled a white hankie out of his pocket, spat on it, bent down and started rubbing my socks trying to remove the stain, but it wouldn't budge.

'I'm not taking you in like that,' he snapped. 'We'll have to go back home.' Then he had second thoughts and gave a big sigh. 'Oh well, we're half way there now,' and we continued towards town, crossing the road so as not to interrupt a group of girls playing hopscotch on the pavement.

When we approached the fountain and old lodging houses where the down and outs lived an unpleasant smell stung my nostrils and I moved to the far side of the pavement. I could see the sad, gaunt faces of occupants with yellow eyes shrunk in their heads peering through dirty windowpanes. Some old men, looking as dirty as the houses they lived in, stood on doorsteps all day long watching people as they passed. I didn't ever speak to the old men and as far as I knew nobody ever did. I wonder what they thought as we walked past; did they know we were going to the gym? Perhaps they did, but didn't care. They spent their lives looking and saying nothing, when they died did anybody care?

Like most other eight year olds I was inquisitive and the questions constantly came from my lips. 'How long were you boxing for Dad?'

'Since I was about your age boy.

'Where did you go to fight Dad?'

'All over Wales boy.'

'Did you make a lot of money boxing?'

'No boy, only the men at the top make a lot of money out of boxing.'

We finally reached the old Angel building that was crumbling and decaying, went through the large wooden front door and up the unlit, musty smelling stairs, fumbling our way towards the room at the top. After what seemed like an age we reached the gym, a grimy, dusty room with cobwebs hanging from a dirty, whitewashed ceiling. But, because I lived in a town full of old and decaying buildings I thought little of the state of the place.

In the gym, one man was skipping. He was running on the spot, as his skipping rope twirled around so fast it was a blur. Other men punched old kit bags stuffed with rags that hung from ceiling rafters, grunting with each punch they threw. A couple of men were sparring, hitting each other for all they were worth in a tiny ring that comprised of four steel corner posts, from which hung three bandage bound ropes. In one corner of the room I spotted two wooden Indian Clubs similar to the ones we had at home that my father used to swing around rhythmically.

My father had explained to me that apart from former British champion Eddie Thomas, who had made a comeback and trained in a room at the 'Bush Hotel', Dowlais, there were no longer active boxers in the Merthyr Valley. Young boys weren't normally allowed in the old Angel Hotel gym, and as was proper, my father asked one of a group of men standing against the boxing ring if it was all right for me to train. The man looked at me disapprovingly, shrugged his shoulders and nodded in reply.

Having got an 'okay' in response to his request, my father took me to a chair and told me to change. It was my introduction to the world of boxing. Who would have thought then that one day I would become a professional boxer? I was taken to a boxing gym to get the feel of boxing. I'd smell the magic of wintergreen oil, and dust rising between floorboards as men skipped and bounced about. There were sounds of men snorting and blowing air through their nostrils as they punched, the squeak of leather boot soles on floor canvas and the vibrating sound of ring ropes as men's bodies bounded against them. There was the squeal of steel as brackets moved against bolts supporting punch bags and the intermittent sound of a bell ringing to start and end rounds. All this put 'boxing' in me. I would become hooked for life on the sounds and smells of a boxing gym.

I changed into my boxing trunks and daps and I believed I was training, but probably just made a nuisance of myself. I watched as my father picked up a skipping rope and said to one of the men standing by the ring, 'Ten minutes, Jack'. The man nodded and looked at the clock he was holding. My father joined the other man and started skipping. The rope went faster and faster until it was almost invisible while my father's feet thudded on the floorboards. After a while the man with the clock shouted, 'Time', and my father stopped skipping and put on a pair of bag gloves. The man shouted 'Time' once more and with a grunt my father punched one of the bags hanging from the ceiling. He threw one, two, three left jabs and a right cross, moved around the bag, jabbed and threw a right cross again. Then, after a while he stood firm and with his two hands held low started fighting the bag, left right, left right, left right he went on and on until the clock man shouted 'Time', and my father stopped.

Sharing the same bottle as the other men my father took a mouthful of water, swilled it around his mouth and spat onto the floor.

Two different men started sparring and one threw a right hand that smashed the other man's nose causing blood to drip onto the floor canvas. They moved around the ring hitting, pulling and holding each other until sweat poured from their faces. Meanwhile someone else started punching the bag.

When my father finished training he wiped himself down with a towel (no showers) and we got dressed again.

'Ready?' asked dad and we headed for the stairs. He always asked me if I was ready even if I'd been waiting for him.

Through my father being known as a boxer I also became known as a boxer, although the only boxing I'd done was playing about at the old Angel Buildings. The boxing tag brought me all kinds of problems with older boys picking fights with me.

My father always told me how important it was not to be a bully and pick fights with anyone. I'd have enough fights with people picking on me and then it was up to me to defend myself.

At home there was a lot of talk about boxing and fighting and we regularly listened to fights on the wireless.

Wales had a number of boxing successes in the form of Swansea's Cliff Curvis, who was to become British

Welterweight Champion and British Heavyweight Champion Johnny Williams from Barmouth, North Wales, who won his title in the same year.

Uncle Will often called and, after complaining to my mother that he was thirsty so that she would make him a cup of tea, he would sit in front of the fire and encourage my father to talk boxing, not that it took much in the way of encouragement. I listened to them discussing the fight my father had outside the Ex-Servicemen's club one Sunday night when he was with his pals. Inside the club, a man about ten years younger than my father had started arguing with one of his pals who was a committee man at the club. My father told the man that it wasn't the time or place to start an argument and he invited my father outside. While my father was taking off his coat someone warned him, 'Watch his head Bill, he's a trouble maker and a rough 'un'.

Outside in the yard, the troublemaker, who had also taken his coat off, rushed at my father who stopped him short with three sharp solid jabs to the face, then crossed a straight right hand punch to his jaw dropping him flat onto his face. He was out like a light.

One night as usual we left home to go to the old Angel Gym. We turned the corner into Plymouth Street and as we were walking towards town someone calling made us turn round. A man of about the same age as my father came up behind us. 'Right, you bastard,' said the man to my father. 'You wouldn't fight me last night, told me to sober up first. Well here I am, let's see how good you are.'

My father looked at the man with distaste, 'Look Archie, I've got the boy with me. It can wait.'

Archie grinned and said, 'Thought as much, no guts. You're a fucking coward.'

My father wasn't one for swearing at anyone and his thoughts were that nobody ever gave him a black eye by swearing at him. Archie stepped forward and jabbed my father in the chest.

''Ang on a minute,' said my father and looked at me. 'George go and stand by the shop door and wait.' I did as told and waited for what I knew was going to be the start of a fight.

Without warning Archie put his head down and rushed into my father taking him back against the wall, then started punching two fisted into my father's stomach. But my father turned him and he fell into the wall. Archie swung with his right hand but my father swayed to one side and the punch hit thin air. Then Archie jumped in with another swing but he tripped and fell to his knees. My father, seeing the opportunity, stepped forward and gave a right uppercut sending Archie up and backwards through the shop window. Glass shattered all over the ground and Archie lay across the windowsill, out for the count. My father caught hold of him by his legs and pulled him out of the window and onto the pavement. As soon as Archie's limp body hit the ground the whole concrete lintel above the window collapsed and crashed down onto the spot where only seconds earlier Archie had been lying.

'Come on George,' said my father and we headed for the old Angel Hotel.

Having climbed the dark dusty stairs to the gym, we arrived to see a boxer arguing with the trainer. 'You said I'd have sparring tonight.'

'I know,' said the trainer. 'I did arrange sparring but he haven't turned up.'

My father walked across and said to the boxer, 'I'll spar with you.'

The boxer, who was half my father's age and twice as big looked in disbelief and said, 'You, you'll spar with me? Come on then Bill, I don't know if you'll do me any good but you can try.'

The trainer gloved my father and the boxer and they started sparring. The younger man waded into my father looking to give him a hiding, but Billy wasn't as easy as he looked and the boxer didn't have it his own way. After a couple of rounds the session got a bit nasty and the fellow who ran the gym, seeing his boxer taking some heavy knocks, ordered the sparring to stop.

'That's enough, no more sparring,' he shouted and started telling my father off. He retaliated and said. 'Look, if he wants to finish it off, we'll go outside.'

The man in charge became agitated and told my father not to go to his gym again.

'I won't,' said my father. 'I'll open my own gym (Billy was determined to have the last word), and I'll let youngsters train there and teach them how to box.'

We both changed into our clothes and without another word left the gym and walked out of the old Angel Buildings.

Chapter 5

To Church

Having become a choirboy at St Tydfil's Parish church I always wondered why hymns were so doleful and depressing. People who went to church feeling happy went home miserable, guilty and sad. Why did everybody whisper in church and why did I get a dirty look if I laughed. I'm sure God didn't mean it to be that way.

Sunday, Sunday, once more Sunday morning had arrived. I awoke hearing my mother call. 'George, come on its time to get up.'

As I moved, my father's old Army greatcoat fell off the bed where my mother had put it on top of the blankets during the night for added warmth. I got out of bed in the cold and ran downstairs to sit in front of the roaring coal fire. My sister, Marilyn, was already down stairs swatting. Mam was fussing about. 'Come on George get washed and don't leave any tidemarks.' I walked to the bosh and cold-water tap in the corner of the kitchen and quickly washed my face, wiped it dry and sat down at the scrubbed top table to eat breakfast. The wireless was on and you can guess what was being played, sad sounding hymns. Mam came into the kitchen and said, 'Go and put your best suit on.' We were due to go to early morning church service and I hated dressing in my one and only best suit because I had to behave myself and not run up the mountain after church or climb the coal tips.

It was a sunny day when I walked out of the back door of 11, Clare Street, through the garden where our chickens scratched the bare ground looking for food and stood in the lane. All of a sudden I heard, 'Ding dong, ding dong, ding dong, ding dong.' The bells of the parish church started ringing. 'Ding dong, ding dong,' what a flaming noise. My mother came out into the garden and I shouted, 'I'll start walking to church.'

'No, wait for your sister,' she ordered, looking at the sun and wishing she could hang out her washing, but never on a Sunday.

'No mun, I'm not walking with any girls, the boys will be playing in the graveyard. I'll join 'im.

'Don't get your best suit dirty,' shouted Mam as I ran up the lane.

Was it my fault if the wind blew coal dust off the tips and covered everything in black grime? Then once more Mam shouted. 'Don't get into any fights with those Caedraw boys. You got your shirt torn last week.'

'It wasn't my bloody fault,' I grumbled to myself. 'They started it.'

'Ding dong ding dong, ding dong ding dong.' Do they have to keep ringing those bells. Why don't they put a wireless on the tower and play music? I turned from time to time looking out for my sister. If the older girls bullied her again I'd pull their hair.

'Ding-dong, ding-dong.' Those infernal bells kept ringing, calling people to church to repent their sins. But I hadn't committed any sins last week so how could I ask God to forgive me. The reply from the vicar to whom I had put the question was, 'Silly boy, of course you have sinned, everybody sins, just being born is a sin.'

I would just have to invent a sin. It was easy for those Catholic boys, they went along to the Catholic Church each week, told the priest any old rubbish and were forgiven. With us it was different, we had to go to church each Sunday and speak directly to God himself.

I reached the main road, Plymouth Street and sat on the wall fronting the community hut, looking across the road at the tin hut that was 'Church of Christ' and forgetting about the dust that would dirty my trousers. People were walking up the main road on their way to the Parish Church and I was daydreaming and whistling. All of a sudden. 'Wallop!' Someone had smacked me across my ear and turning quickly I could see my Bopa. 'You have been told before not to whistle on a Sunday,' she said, and off she strode.

'George, you'll be late for church.' I turned to see Mrs Thomas as she walked past on her way to join the righteous group. Then I had an idea, thinking about the delicious Cox's Pippins that hung on the trees in Mrs Thomas's garden. If, by climbing over the wall and pinching apples I could be sinful, then it would serve a purpose.

But, wait a minute there are the Caedraw boys, why worry about sins anyway. I jumped off the wall and strolled towards the church. The vicar was standing on the church step giving a smile and saying, 'Hello' to his congregation. By the time I'd reached the church gate the Caedraw boys had been scootaddled by the vicar for jumping on the gravestones. There'd be no confrontation with them for me.

I walked past the vicar and he stared at me. In return, I looked at him as if to say, 'What?' and went straight into the vestry along with the other boys and put my Cassock on.

'Are we all ready?' asked the choirmaster. No one replied.

'Right let's go then,' he said and walked behind us, watching to make sure we sat in the correct order. I avoided looking at Gareth because last week he had made me laugh in the middle of prayers and I'd had a row from the choirmaster. The service ended and I left before the vicar took his usual position by the entrance to eyeball anyone who he thought hadn't put a donation in the collection box. I waited outside for

Marilyn and we walked home together, stopping every so often to stand over one of the iron grids on the pavement that gave light to someone's cellar. We'd try and see if any money had been accidentally dropped down, not that we could do anything to retrieve the dosh anyway. After kicking a stone all the way down the back lane I followed Marilyn through the garden gate.

When we entered our house Mam said, 'George take off your best suit and put your old clothes on.

'Oh, it's not worth it now I'll change later on.'

'Do as you're told, tell 'im Bill.'

'Do as you're told,' said my father sternly, 'Change your clothes.'

But I was stubborn and answered, 'No, I'm not.'

I only got to wear my best suit once a week so why couldn't I wear it for a while longer. Besides, it's an awful lot of work changing.

'Do as you're told or I'll smack you,' said my father.

Reluctantly I climbed the stairs to change, muttering to myself. There was a knock on the front door and Mam answered, 'George it's Raymond. Are you going out?' I grabbed my coat, and followed by Raymond walked out through the garden into the back lane where Walter Hale was leading his horse and cart. A couple of times each week Walter travelled around the back lanes delivering coal, but today the poor horse was struggling to pull the cart over-laden with iron rails. As they passed, I pulled one of the rails making it fall and Walter chased me up the lane as far as the railway arches (known as the oakies) where he gave up and walked back shouting abuse as he went.

I waited for Ray. 'You were lucky,' he said. 'You'll probably get a wallop if he tells your father.' I shrugged my shoulders and walked on. No point in worrying until I got home.

Later when I was heading for home I wondered why nobody gave thought to the poor horse pulling the heavy cart.

There should be law that anyone who made a horse pull an over laden cart should be made to pull it themselves and if they refused be made to lie on the ground and let the horse urinate over them.

We wandered over to the main road and sat on the wall outside the community hut. On the doorstep of the house opposite, once the Mountain Ash Inn, was Maggie (Peg leg) Morgan, a small woman who stood on the doorstep of her house most of the day watching people and traffic go past. She was known to have a sharp tongue and could frequently be heard quarrelling with someone passing. Maggie hobbled about on one leg and a wooden crutch. I never did understand why Maggie was called 'peg leg' when she didn't have a wooden leg.

After allowing time for Walter to disappear I went home the back way along the dirt lane where earlier he had chased me, passed underfed sheep scraping barren gardens for food. I arrived at our house and on entering the kitchen could see my father preparing to kill one of the chickens reared in our back garden. Bought as chicks, they were fattened up on scraps of food and then on special occasions the poor souls were slaughtered. My father used a surgeon's knife which he smoothed over a stone until razor sharp.

'Don't touch the knife,' I was warned as I looked at it longingly, wishing I could borrow it to cut sticks.

A week before Christmas wire netting was put around the legs of the kitchen table and the chickens kept inside in case somebody tried to pinch them. My father would grab a luckless chicken ready to kill for dinner, sit on a chair with a bucket on the floor between his legs and put the chicken between his knees, 'Hold still you bugger,' he'd say and cut the chicken's jugular vein and the bird would slowly bleed to death.

Mam joined us in the kitchen. 'It's your fault,' she said to my father.

'I'm not bothered,' said Dad. 'They can do what they like.'

'What's the matter?' I asked.

'Nothing,' said Mam. 'Nothing to do with you.'

'What's the matter,' I asked again. 'Tell me.'

My father stopped what he was doing. 'Oh it's just that I was coming home from the Labour Club last Saturday when I saw Mary Ann Lewis, who lives next door to your Bopa in Plymouth Street, standing against a wall in a compromising position with some man. I told your Bopa about it. She couldn't keep her mouth shut and told a neighbour who then told Mary Ann's husband. There'll be all hell let loose now.' My father carried on plucking the chicken.

'What's a compromising position?' I asked.

Suddenly there was a load rat-tat-tat at the door and I followed my father to see who was knocking. Standing on the pavement outside was a small group of people. Ben Lewis stood in front with his hand on the shoulder of Mary Ann, his wife, who he prodded forward, then poked his finger at my father. 'Right Billy Evans, tell us, did you or did you not see my wife in a compromising position with another man?'

There was a moment's silence while the gathering waited tensely for a reply.

'Yes I did,' said my father, and the group of people moved towards him.

But my father was prepared. He picked up Mary Ann and using her as a battering ram forced his intended attackers back onto the road where they collapsed in a heap. As quick as a flash we ran into our house, slammed the door shut and listened while the crowd outside had some sort of meeting before leaving. We heard no more of it.

Oh well, back out to play. Meeting Michael and Ypres, named after a famous First World War battle in Belgium, we decided to cross the railway viaduct to get to Rhydycar. Ypres, whose own trousers were being washed had had to borrow his father's, and he clutched at the waist to stop them falling down. We climbed the wooden style, up the bank onto the railway line and began walking across the viaduct that spanned the railway goods yard and river Taff to Rhydycar. Suddenly someone shouted, 'Oi, stop.'

We turned to see a railway policeman running in our direction. Without hesitation we took off across the viaduct but Ypres's feet kept getting caught in the legs of his father's trousers which were too long for him. 'Carry on boys,' yelled Ypres who had been forced to stop. When we turned we could see the copper holding Ypres by the collar. That afternoon I was sitting at home when there was a knock on the door and I looked up as my mother led the policeman into the kitchen. Ypres, when asked who the other boys were, had given fictitious names. But by putting two and two together it hadn't taken the copper long to find Michael and me.

Chapter 6

Back in the Gym

There was a chance for me to avoid the daily boredom when my father, being a determined man, started his own boxing gym by renting the Old Drill Hall in Georgetown, Merthyr. And so began Merthyr Tydfil Amateur Boxing Club. I was still only nine years old and boxing training was just a night out for me.

With the opening of the Merthyr ABC, boxing was reintroduced to the valley, giving young lads the chance to learn the art of boxing. These lads might otherwise never have laced on a pair of boxing gloves. Fathers came to the Gym with their young sons, thinking back to the days when Merthyr had been a hub of boxing activity and famous boxers had displayed their talents in the valley town.

From all the young boys training it was easy to distinguish between the pretentious, 'run-of-the-mill' tryers, and the naturals who had the makings of good boxers. The naturals only had to be shown boxing moves a couple of times before they became automatic, while others just couldn't get the 'knack'. Youngsters were shown how to jab, using their body weight as a coiled spring to lever force behind each punch. The trick is to get within range and throw a punch without your opponent realizing it. Many boxers 'telegraph' their punches enabling the opponent to avoid or block them. Boxing techniques had to be explained; things like how the dangers of leading with a right hand (providing you're boxing orthodox and not southpaw), which leave you open to a right counterpunch to the heart or solar plexus and a left hook to the jaw.

Hitting correctly is natural in boxers, but delivering the punch can be learnt. The technique of hitting is something boxers are born with, they've either got it or they haven't. It is the reason why some boxers can deliver a knockout punch while others can't. One such young natural boxer was Howard Winstone, who, thanks initially to Billy Evans and Merthyr ABC eventually brought the World Featherweight Championship home to Wales. Many other boys were taught how to box by Billy Evans and some went on to become good professional boxers. I doubt very much, whether my father (or anyone else for that matter) thought at the time that starting Merthyr ABC would result in Merthyr eventually becoming recognized world wide for its boxing talents. It is the amateur trainers who are the mainstay of boxing, nurturing young lads from raw novices and helping to produce the qualities of champions.

Without doubt, the backbone of boxing is the amateur trainer, in the gym every night for no financial reward, interested only in the young boxers' welfare, hoping they will first become amateur, then professional champions. The proud feeling when the young lad, taught boxing by the amateur trainer succeeded in the chosen sport was all my father ever wanted.

Merthyr ABC regularly promoted boxing shows in Merthyr and also toured the country, taking boxers to different venues. Once again Merthyr became established in boxing and many young boxers with Merthyr ABC became amateur champions. Transport to shows was usually provided by one of the men who helped in the gym. Normally Billy sat in the front passenger seat next to the driver, while about eight of us boxers crammed into the back. The overloaded car would struggle up the side of Rhigos Mountain and Billy would start one of his many stories. 'I remember the time I put a professional boxing show on at the Old Drill Hall Merthyr,' he'd say. 'The hall was full of spectators waiting for the show to start. We were waiting for one of the top of the bill fighters to arrive and when he finally turned up, demanded more money or he wouldn't box. After a long argument and calling the boxer names for reneging on the agreement I was forced to pay him the extra. Another show I lost money on.'

But for my father, running the gym at the Drill Hall, Georgetown was a bind. Two gym nights each week we'd have to arrive early and assemble the gear before the boxers arrived, and then, when the gym session had finished, take all the gear down again. A condition of renting the hall was that we left it as we found it. Then my grandfather, George Aris, as secretary of the Merthyr Labour Club provided Billy with an opportunity to rent the club's old concert hall and the Merthyr Amateur Boxing Club had a new gym.

The Labour Club Boxing Gym thrived three nights a week and my father and his mates had their hands full controlling all the young boxers. Skipping is one of the best exercises, but for most newcomers it took a while to do this properly. For a long time boys would turn the rope trying to get the knack, then suddenly success, the skipping rope swung around without their feet getting caught in it.

'How much longer Bill?' some kid would ask.

My father would look at his watch and urge the boys on by saying, 'Come on boys, 'aven't got long to go.' Then he'd say, 'Ten seconds,' and the boys skipped as fast as they could until the shout of, 'Time!'

All sorts of kids wanted to box, most never made it. A lot of fathers would be hanging around the gym watching their sons training. Some of the boys were dressed in flash new gear while others wore whatever they could find. There were the no hopers who tried hard but never made it, and the middle of the road lads who were sort of average. There were the boys who didn't miss a night's training and could box well in the gym, but when matched to box in a show they wouldn't turn up; had got a cold or flu, any excuse not to box. Half a dozen or so boys were very good boxers, always in the gym and always turned up for fights.

By now I'd slotted into the world of boxing but I suffered an accident that meant I was invalided for a long time. Along with Michael Barry and my cousin Lawrence I found myself wandering along the old tramroad at the bottom of Merthyr. We came across two pretty young girls a little older than ourselves at an age when our hormones were telling us to take an interest. The two girls were foreigners, all the way from Bristol, visiting friends or family in Merthyr. Of course, the girls didn't want to know three scruffy lads, but not to be deterred we followed them doing a bit of showing off. We thought we'd head them off and run to the top of an old bridge parapet where, unfortunately, I lost my balance and fell, landing feet first on the tarmac road below, in front of the two girls.

Instead of running away, the two girls picked me up and one holding me by the legs and the other my shoulders carried me home as Michael and Lawrence walked behind. On reaching our house in Clare Street, the girls knocked on the door which was opened by my mother. She was well used to me being involved in accidents but this time I'd broken bones in both ankles. My mother gave the two girls sixpence each, thanked them for their kind act and we didn't ever see them again.

It was 1953 when I began my many visits to hospital with both my legs encased in plaster of Paris up to my knee. With cracked bones in both ankles I had to walk with the aid of crutches. I was housebound for the first time in my life and it was something I couldn't adjust to. I was ten years old and on my last year at Caedraw School. The topic of conversation was the forthcoming eleven plus examination, the outcome of which decided where a child was to be slotted for secondary education.

I failed the exam and was assigned to Queen's Road Secondary Modern School.

There was an addition to our family when my brother Billy was born. My new brother was a nice kid and I thought the world of him, but the trouble was I had to look after the little terror. Getting out of the house when Billy started walking was difficult because he always wanted to come with me where ever I was going, and it usually meant my pal Michael and me tip toeing out of the house so that he wouldn't hear us and sneaking off to the centre, where I played snooker. I mean like, how could I be a dedicated lay-about if I couldn't practice playing snooker? After many good years at the Merthyr Labour Club producing boxing champions, club members complained that dust created by boxers training fell onto snooker tables in the room below the gym and my father was asked to leave. He then rented the gymnasium at the Merthyr YMCA.

Chapter 7

Queen's Road School

As if life wasn't bad enough!

The year was 1954 and the day arrived when I was to continue my education at Queen's Road Secondary Modern School. Leaving our house I walked across to the main road and climbed the mountain slope, through the streets of Twynyrodyn to Thomastown Park and Queen's Road. I joined others shuffling along Queen's Road in a stunned silence, until we arrived at the school and I stood by one of two iron gates that fronted driveways leading uphill between areas of untidy laurel bushes. At the top of the driveways, looking forebodingly down were two single story buildings. In front of one building a teacher swiped a cane against his trouser leg that seemed to indicate, 'Watch it.' Along with others I trudged my way to the top of one of the drives feeling a little nervous but at the same time excited. All the other kids were strangers to me, and the older boys walked around with authority. You could tell they knew the score. The school comprised of two main buildings, one marked 'Girls', the other 'Boys', although both sexes were taught together. Since it was not yet starting time, the pupils walked around the yards and among them the new kids looked lost. No school uniforms were worn at Secondary Modern schools, instead all types of clothing was seen and footwear varied from boots, shoes, daps or rubber wellies. Poor kids stood out like a sore thumb.

A whistle was blown and we were told to go to the main hall of one school building. Standing at one end of the hall on each side of the headmaster were the teachers. The Headmaster, Ernie Hughes, who looked deadly serious, was a small man with a shiny top to his head and spectacles hanging from the end of his nose that he continually pushed up. That first confrontation with the teachers and the verbal instructions from the headmaster were at the very least, intimidating and at the end of assembly my impression was that some of the pupils were on the verge of crying, some were almost suicidal. Then, just as we were all about to collapse with horror, we were ordered to go to different classrooms. I have a feeling that when all the kids left the hall the teachers rolled about laughing. Every morning was the same with Ernie staring at the hall full of pupils daring anyone to smile or laugh. I recall one occasion when he shouted at one pupil. 'What are you smiling at boy, how dare you, see me in my room later.'

We were ordered to report to Miss Morris, our form teacher, in a classroom at the start of the corridor. We waited for our first lesson that was all about, 'getting to know you.' New kids were placed in a class according to their ability and I was put in 1Q, the top first year class. If I thought I was privileged and going to be taught something then I was mistaken. Suddenly the classroom door opened and in strode Miss Morris, an elderly looking, little lady with a wrinkled face of harsh Dickension appearance whose bark proved to be worse than her bite. She was unable to smile, or so it seemed, but worked hard enough and meant well. After a period of boring dialogue a bell would ring to signal the end of the lesson and we'd make our way to the next classroom where, according to our timetables Social Studies was taught.

The Social Studies teacher, Ozzie Bevan, worked hard, commanded attention and respect and to make sure of this he always kept a big stick within easy reach. Ozzie was a short man with a severe, granite-like look on his face. He limped, as a result of a war wound, it was said he had a terrible temper, and it was accepted that whenever his face was like thunder his leg was playing up. I'd sit looking at Ozzie and wonder, was he a German spy, or maybe Hitler himself? Was his limp the result of carrying a rifle down the leg of his trousers? All teachers should display a C.V. on the notice board for pupils to see, saving hours of pointless speculation.

The sound of the dinner bell always created a stampede of pupils towards the school canteen, and a queue quickly formed with everyone pushing and elbowing their way towards the door. Older and bigger boys who were normally the better fighters being first, my position was halfway down the line of hungry pupils. After what seemed like an age, the male teacher on canteen duty came outside and said, 'Right you lot, no running, no talking.' Then he opened the canteen door and quickly stepped back to avoid being trampled on.

The first boys through the door sat nearest the serving hatch and were first in the queue for food. After dinner had been served the teacher on duty had a word with the canteen staff and if there was any food left over he'd look at the pupils and say, 'Right who wants seconds?' Half the kids in the hall raised their hands in the air. The teacher would point his cane and say, 'First four boys,' and the four nearest the hatch carried their plates for a second helping. If there was any food still remaining the teacher pointed his stick again, 'Right next two,' and a couple more kids went for seconds. By this time the extra food had gone and I kept thinking, 'That's not fair, us younger boys should be allowed to have seconds.'

The following day I joined the rush for the canteen and was pushed back down the waiting queue outside the canteen door. The teacher gave his usual speech, opened the door and jumped out of the way. Once inside, older boys took up the first six chairs and before food was served one boy went to the serving hatch to see what was for dinner. Like a flash I left my seat, ran down the aisle and sat in his chair. The older boy ran back and started to shake the chair with me sitting on it saying, 'Get out, George. It's my chair.' But George wasn't going to budge as the older boy kept shaking the chair and all the boys started shouting, 'Fight, fight.' The teacher, who would normally have waded in with his cane quickly walked out of the canteen as Tom and I tore into each other. Later Tom and I were called separately to the teachers' room. He told me that he had waited a long time for someone to give Tom the bully a hiding. I was told to hold my hand out and given two light taps for fighting. Fighting was a regular occurrence among the boys and the shout of, 'Fight', saw the pupils forming a crowd around the fighters until a teacher came upon the scene. As usual, the bigger the boy the more respect he got. Smaller boys like myself were regularly in scraps.

There was still one small glimmer of hope for the first year pupils of Queen's Road School when half a dozen pupils, thought to be the brightest were transferred to Quaker's Yard Technical School. There was a good chance for me and a few other pupils. But our suspicions were aroused when one teacher started to praise pupils who were so dull they should never have been in the first class anyway. When it was announced who was to go to Quaker's Yard, it was obvious some parents were more influential than others.

Okay, so maybe I'm biased, perhaps I wouldn't have qualified for Quaker's Yard. But the position remained the same, the majority of pupils at Queen's Road school had to stay there and rot for four years. I would have to stay at Queen's Road and at the end be no more literate than when I started. I've no doubt that because of the system regarding the daily care of pupils, teachers slipped into the same thought pattern and turned up at Queen's Road school just to be paid. But I always thought that a number of teachers (even considering the doleful regime) did their best at teaching to the standards that they were allowed.

When the bell sounded to end school for the day, it was a quick run home to have tea before delivering evening newspapers, for which I received fifteen shillings a week that I handed to my mother. I was allowed to keep any tips I received when collecting the paper money on Friday. I'd wait at Merthyr Railway Station for the train to arrive from Cardiff with a delivery of *South Wales Echo* evening newspapers. With a bag full of *Echos* slung over my shoulder I'd start my round through town and along Bridge Street that bordered the river Taff, where I'd wait outside the Greyhound public house to see if the results of drinking cider caused fights. Frequently men and women would pile out onto the road pulling hair and punching each other. Then onto Caedraw, where a group of men waited to borrow an *Echo* to see the horseracing results. As I approached the men I'd hear one shout, ''Ang on son give us a quick look at an *Echo*.'

'You'll have to buy one, butt,' I'd say.

'But we only want to see the results.'

I'd reluctantly hand them an *Echo*, and wait until they'd passed it around before getting it back.

One night it was pouring with rain when I began my delivering journey. The bag was heavy and I frequently stopped to ease the strap digging into my shoulder. I was approaching Caedraw and the same motley crew of gamblers was waiting to borrow an *Echo*. But this evening I was in no mood to wait and as one of the men started to ask I quickly said, 'Look mister, if you want to read the results you'll have to buy a paper.' There was a moment's silence, then one of the gang said, 'Okay, sell me one then.'

'Sorry I don't have any spare.'

That last statement got me a lot of abuse and one of the gang shouted after me. 'You cheeky little fucker, don't come around here again.'

Unfortunately, during my time at school the Education Authority no longer encouraged boxing, but the Merthyr ABC was active with many talented amateur boxers. Howard Winstone was the young amateur champion everyone was talking about, talented, with great prospects, sixteen years old and winning all his amateur contests in style. Winstone had joined my father's gym at eleven years of age and after five years had achieved many successes including winning the Welsh and British Schoolboy Championships. Howard Winstone was coming to the age when he'd want to turn professional, and whoever was fortunate enough to sign the Merthyr marvel would be securing fame and fortune. Looking on from the wings was former British champion, Eddie Thomas, who had opened his own gym at Penydarren, on the outskirts of Merthyr town, and encouraged Winstone and other boxers to leave the Merthyr ABC and join his new Boxing Club.

My father knew that Howard Winstone would one day turn professional, and when Winstone announced as much he encouraged him on that quest. Billy Evans had no hand in who Winstone chose as manager, but who better, he thought, than Merthyr man Eddie Thomas who knew the pro game and would train Winstone as he had once trained himself. Howard Winstone continued his success in the amateur ranks achieving a gold medal in the Empire games in Cardiff. Then the news came that Howard Winstone had trapped his right hand in a machine at work and lost the tips of his fingers. What a tragedy, there was concern that the Merthyr boxing prodigy wouldn't be able to use his right hand again and would have to stop boxing.

Boxing in South Wales at that time was on the up, with Abercynon's Dai Dower first becoming Commonwealth Flyweight Champion, and then winning the British and European Championships. Cardiff heavyweight, Joey Erskine, claimed national honours by winning the British and Commonwealth championships.

In the meantime, Merthyr ABC continued. I was boxing

regularly and joined the Army Cadet Force, whose headquarters was situated in the grounds of the Drill Hall, Merthyr, where my father had started the first Merthyr Amateur Boxing Club. I entered the ACF boxing championships and boxed through the eliminators at different venues throughout the country, winning the British finals at Aldershot Army barracks. At Aldershot, I tasted life in the regular Army for the first time. One morning I woke to the sound of someone shouting and looking out of the window, I could see soldiers marching outside in the freezing cold. Perhaps Army life wasn't for me after all.

At this time, my sister Marilyn became the first girl from Merthyr to be accepted to London University, with the assistance of Merthyr Tydfil Council who in their wisdom chose to help the Borough's talented schoolkids from poorer families by providing grants. My parents had no telephone or transport and the thought of Marilyn going to London was as if she was going to the other end of the world. Grandfather George Aris asked if he could have the honour of escorting Marilyn to London by train while my brother Billy, my mother, father and I stood at the end of Clare Street to wave to my sister and Grandfather as the train thundered past on its journey to London.

One night at the YMCA gym we were surprised by the arrival of Howard Winstone, who, ever cheerful, acknowledged those present and started speaking to my father. The boys stopped training and gathered around. Winstone was upset and explained that Eddie Thomas had told him to stay away from training and rest for some months in the hope that he'd regain the use of his right hand, because a one handed fighter was no good and Winstone would have to consider finishing boxing. Winstone showed us the injured fingers of his right hand and it was difficult to imagine him using his right fist as a formidable weapon in boxing again. But my father had faith in the talented Winstone who already had a good left jab, and suggested that he concentrate on his left hand to compensate for his injured right hand. Winstone asked my father if he'd train him in secret at the YMCA. So, night after night, week after week, Howard Winstone arrived early at the YMCA, gym where my father coached him, encouraging him to concentrate on using his already talented left jab. Although past forty years of age, my father sparred with Winstone until his right hand had healed well enough, then all the boys in the gym sparred with Winstone in his mission to cultivate his left jab. And so, the magical left jab of Howard Winstone was formed. Eventually, it was time for Howard Winstone to return to the Penydarren Gym where Eddie Thomas put the professional touches to the already cultured left jab.

At this time we had an addition to the family when my youngest brother Wayne was born. Oh boy, yet another brother for me to look after.

Chapter 8

Back at School

Back at Queen's Road school we were all meditating under the planned mis-guidance of teachers.

Maths teacher was Mr Bow. With respect to me as a pupil, he failed in his job. Often, he made me and my classmates play silly games, 'O'Grady says' being his favourite. English lessons were slightly more interesting. During one lesson a boy asked the teacher. 'Please sir, are you going to give us homework?' This was our third year at Queen's Road School, and so far no homework had been given to any pupil in my class. The teacher stood up and walked over to the boy. 'What, did I hear you ask for homework?'

Looking sheepish the boy said, 'Yes sir.'

The teacher rounded on him. 'Give you homework? Who told you to ask for homework? You can't do your work in school time never mind homework.' I can imagine the English teacher entering the staff room at break time and saying to the other teachers, 'You must listen to this one, a boy in my last class asked for homework.' I would not have been surprised if one of the other teachers said, 'What? I hope you punished him?'

The next lesson was Physical Education taken by tall, athletic looking Bill Evans (back trouble) who tried his best and the pupils respected him. When all the boys had settled in the gym Bill said, 'Today boys we're going to the school vegetable garden where the ancient Gorsedd stones are.'

I thought, 'Oh aye, what's going on here, then.'

The 'garden' Bill Evans spoke about was a piece of waste ground adjacent to the school, in the centre of which was a circle of large stones. Arriving at the ground Bill Evans started to reminisce. 'Oh yes, at one time this patch of ground was a garden where the pupils worked hard cultivating vegetables.' That seemed all right I thought. Spend a bit of school time growing veg to take home, nice one. Then Bill Evans spoiled my thoughts. 'All the vegetables grown in this garden were given to the canteen to cook for school dinners.' What a downer, work hard for months digging and growing veg and the canteen took it all to cook for school dinners. Sod that for a lark. It was as if Bill Evans could read my thoughts. 'Don't you think it's a good idea to give the veg to the canteen, boys?'

'Yes sir, a good idea.'

Then one of the boys asked, 'Are we going to do any gardening today sir?' Bill started to scratch his head, 'Oh, er, um, no I don't think it will be possible, I haven't got the time. Right, lesson over, all start walking back to the hall and no talking.' Well, that was a good lesson on gardening. We didn't ever go there again.

The woodwork teacher, Ken Davies, was a pleasant enough fellow, short, stocky and bald headed (another of the war wounded) who enjoyed talking. What a pity the talking wasn't about woodwork. During most of the woodwork lessons we were told to sit on our benches and pay attention. Usually the topic would be Ken's wartime experiences. Ken mentioned that he personally didn't suffer at the hands of the Japanese. His plight was having to drink infested water which gave him dysentery. Now, I'm not trying to make light of his predicament; jungle warfare couldn't have been pleasant and I know he suffered in later life. The first two or three times he told the story was interesting, but four years of the same story?

Ken's misfortune would eventually lead to my misfortune too.

Metalwork, and the teacher's name was Ernie Bonfield, a tall thin man with a lean sallow face and a bald head who always stooped, never smiled and seemed to me to shake his head every time he looked at me. It was the same situation as in woodwork. Once again, the teacher liked the sound of his own voice and we were told to sit on workbenches that were soaked with oil, did it matter if our clothes became soiled? The metalwork building housed lathes, drills and other machinery that were rarely used in my presence by Bonfield. No pupil, even under supervision, ever used the machines in my presence. Lo and behold another continuous story. No germ infested water this time. With Bonfield it was a case of smoking too many fags for too long. Pupils had to sit and listen to the perils of smoking that eventually lead to Mr Bonfield requiring stomach surgery. Once again we were back to keeping the pupils occupied and not taught anything of substance. Not one of the boys was taught enough about woodwork or metalwork to be able to seek a job in those areas on leaving school.

There was a lack of the encouragement needed, to enable pupils to try and achieve something which would provide them with a future other than labouring. The school seemed to be staffed by war wounded and I think that at least one of the teachers was mentally deficient. Ninety percent of the teachers at Queen's Road would probably not have been allowed to teach today. I can imagine a conversation at an interview for teaching posts where the interviewer would be saying to an applicant, 'Don't worry, if you fail at this interview there's always Queen's Road.'

The teachers were probably poorly qualified. Given the often-lacklustre way in which a subject was taught, it was obvious that they adopted a thoroughly indifferent attitude. In my opinion, certain teachers were generally inept.

Merthyr Tydfil is a large industrial area and factories were continually encouraged to come to the South Wales Valleys and bring work with them. But, before companies would settle in Merthyr they had to be guaranteed lots of unskilled labour. No doubt other incentives had to be considered, but without a steady supply of factory hands (factory fodder) setting up in Merthyr would have been pointless. This was the age of aquiescence for the majority of pupils at Secondary Modern Schools. For many years school leavers were happy to have a lifetime of work even though it was usually labouring. But what a shame! In my opinion, those in authority were short sighted in not foreseeing or not wanting to foresee the decline in industry, which would leave thousands of people unemployed and not qualified to do any other work. As the years rolled by, we were to witness the effects of recession. Without a reasonable education to enable people to find employment elsewhere, they were destined to form queues outside the Job Centre. I wonder if there was any guilt in the minds of the teaching authorities?

After four years at Queen's Road school, I left with little academic knowledge of any kind. We were taught how to read and write well enough to be able to complete a simple job application form, though my handwriting was so bad that I couldn't read it, and I'd been placed in the top form! I can only imagine the plight of pupils placed in lower forms. It became clear to me as time went on that having to mention Queen's Road School on a job application form categorised me. If someone applied for a job any higher than a labourer, the sight of Queen's Road written under the heading of school and I imagined the employer automatically disregarding the application. The fact was that the school system must have been as boring for the teachers as for the pupils. Because there were no significant exams at the end of each term, pupils had no incentive to try. Possibly, teachers, realising the situation, towards the end of the day would start glancing at their watches, take deep breaths and look out of the window to make sure the world was still there. But there you are, that was how it happened. It was 1958, and I left school and entered the big wide world.

At Merthyr ABC I started missing training until eventually, joining my mates, I preferred going to dances and pubs and was more interested in girls than training. My father closed the gym.

Chapter 9

Work at Guest Keen

Through a meeting and an informal interview with the manager, I was given a job in the office of Guest Keen Iron and Steel Works, Dowlais (known as the Ivor Works). Here, for centuries, iron and steel had been forged and transported all over the world. Mainly through the development of industry and the influx of workers, Dowlais became a large area of cottages, shopping areas, pubs, clubs, chapels and churches, which formed a town for mainly mine and steelworkers.

Three weeks after leaving school, I rose early on an April day in 1958 when I was to start my first working day at the Steelworks. My father had already left for work at the Imperial Chemical Industries, Dowlais, where he was a painter, and I thought about how he arrived home with aching arms having brushed paint onto large steel tanks all day long. On a Friday he handed his meagre pay packet to my mother saying that ICI would give their workers anything bar money. Still, this was to be the day when I started full time employment and in my eyes became a man. I finished breakfast and left home to walk the two miles into Merthyr town centre where corporation buses began their journeys. Climbing onto a bus with Dowlais marked on the front I asked the time of departure and arrival at Guest Keen, Dowlais before buying a ticket. At the back of my mind was Dad's advice, 'Whatever you do don't be late for work.' While travelling I daydreamed about the world of Steel making in the nineteenth century. I pictured men that were overworked and underpaid with sweat running from their tired limbs as they shielded their eyes from the glare of molten metal, and a foreman shouting, 'Dai you're fired,' because he sat to rest a weary body. Office workers received the same treatment, only they had to spend the day tied to a desk.

On a Friday the fatigued workmen lined up to be handed their pittance of a wage in cash and beer chits for working overtime that could only be exchanged in public houses owned by Guest Keen. The same men arrived home in the evening to a cottage rented from their employer who owned most of Dowlais, to eat a meal cooked by the slave called a wife, and then, after bathing in hot water also prepared by the wife he would spend the rest of the evening in the pub, drinking beer in order to redeem his beer chits.

With no home luxuries life was hard and cold for families and stories were told about men who worked and drank themselves to death. It has been calculated, that in the nineteenth century there were over two hundred unlicensed public houses in Dowlais along with company owned pubs. Owing to their time at work in appalling conditions it is little wonder men spent a lifetime suffering from infected lungs, burst eardrums, arthritic limbs and other illnesses. 'Was this a life I was prepared to accept?'

All of a sudden, I was brought back to the present by the bus shuddering to a halt outside Guest Keen Iron and Steel. I alighted and, overawed at the sight before me, stared at the massive world famous Iron and Steel works. There was smoke rising from chimneystacks and a general drone coming from the large housings, while bumping could be heard as railway wagons were shunted by locos. Men walked about the works while others appeared to be working.

A little nervous I walked to the security lodge, opened the

large wooden door and peeped inside. 'Come in,' said one of the two old men who sat in a room sectioned off from the passage. I quietly entered the room that consisted of Victorian type furniture and could see the old men, one whose head was as bald as a coot and the other wearing a trilby seated on chairs that had years of use etched into them.

'Excuse me, sir, I'm here to start work,' I said, smiling but getting no response. Once again Dad's words rang in my ear, 'Always say, "sir".'

'What's your name?' the same old gent that asked me to come in muttered.

'George Evans, sir.'

'Where do you live?'

'11, Clare Street, Merthyr Tydfil.'

The door opened and a big man whose head also sported a trilby walked in, stared at me for a moment with a face that had the impressive look of a policeman and said, 'I'm Thomas, Head of Security, what do you want?'

'I'm here to start work, sir.'

'O yes, what's your name?'

'George Evans, sir.'

'Where do you live?'

'11, Clare Street, Merthyr, sir.' I'm getting fed up now.

'Sit there,' said Mr Thomas pointing to an empty chair. He picked up the telephone and after a short conversation pointed in the direction of the general office. 'Go to the reception and tell them who you are.' Then, changing his mind he said, 'I'd better come with you to show you the way.'

I followed Thomas who strode along with a gait of authority, swinging his arms in marching fashion as he walked up the drive. We stepped over railway lines passing locos shunting wagons loaded with large steel objects, arrived at the main office block and entered through a large doorway into a long corridor with wooden block flooring. The manager's secretary asked me to follow her to an office where Works Manager, Ted

Yorath greeted me, shook my hand and welcomed me to the Ifor works.

Short, thickset with a bald patch on top of his head, Yorath was a genuine person to whom I owe a lot. A quick chat and Yorath introduced me to accountant Bill Cockburn who stood over six feet tall, a big man who spoke with a Scottish accent, had an air of authority and smiled as we shook hands. Cockburn introduced me to other employees before finally entering the cost and accounts department where a dozen workers were employed. Len Davies, who sat at the first desk, was bald and portly, always making wisecracks and unfunny jokes that the staff felt obliged to laugh at. He'd say, "Ave you 'eard the one about the vicar and the actress.' As one, they would all lift their heads and laugh. Then Len would say, "Ang on, I haven't finished the joke yet.'

The first couple of days found me sitting with Bill Cockburn being shown basic office work, and then I was given a desk in the Cost and Accounts Dept.

My work consisted of, 'inking in' which meant writing in pen over work someone else had written in pencil. I was apprehensive at first because of my poor handwriting, but I soon discovered with relief, that some of the office worker's handwriting was worse than mine. Half a dozen desks were placed in the centre of the room with Len sitting at one end and me the other. Most written work was completed in pencil in case a mistake was made. This could then be rubbed out, but I could never understand why there was only one rubber to share between all the accounts' staff.

'Who's got the rubber?' Someone would ask and the others would look under newspapers and other items.

'Roy you 'ad the rubber.'

'No I 'aven't got it, John 'ad it last.'

'Look on the floor it might 'ave fallen off the table.'

All the work completed by accounts staff was calculated and checked by a 'comptometer operator', a girl whose sole purpose was, by means of a machine, to check the work and put a rubber stamp on to signify 'correct'. Then it was passed to me to go over in ink, or by some clerks who preferred to ink in their own work rather than sit doing nothing.

I sat at the end desk waiting for work to be handed down to me and my gaze must have wandered around the room a thousand times. Boy, was this job boring. Suddenly I was brought back to the present when a voice said, 'George, ink this in?' I took the sheet of paper off Jim and looked at the rows of pencilled figures. Okay, here goes.

Ten minutes later I'd finished copying over in pen and handed it back. The clerk I handed the work to looked amazed. 'That was quick, George,' he said. 'Ink it over again to make sure.' I looked down at the sheet of paper. Hell-a-man, inking in is inking in for God's sake, how could I do it wrong?

I picked up the pen and once again copied over the work I had already completed. By the time I'd finished (ten minutes later) the writing was so bold it occurred to me that if I went over it again the pen would go right through the paper. But it didn't take long to dawn on me that appearing to be busy while doing nothing was an art, an apprenticeship, to be learned over a number of years. But how did they cope with the boredom? Perhaps that was also part of the learning?

Suddenly, Len quipped another joke and John stared and blinked, trying to fathom out the punch line, while Christine rolled her eyes towards the ceiling and said, 'Can't you think of any new jokes?'

Each clerk would in turn leave their desks, only to hot foot it back when footsteps that might be one of the managers could be heard approaching the office. Some of the staff took advantage of having little to do by swotting for exams they didn't get around to sitting, while members of Dowlais Male Voice Choir hummed songs in preparation for a concert. It got to the stage where I thought Len had been employed just to keep the others from falling asleep.

The clerks stayed at their desks leaning on elbows supporting chins in the palm of their hands. Every time somebody started to nod off Len began talking to them and they'd come awake muttering, 'What, what, what,' and rubbing their eyes.

I was employed alongside people who, having worked for many years in the same environment had become inured and at the age of sixty-five retired, collected their long service watches, walked out of the works gates and dropped dead soon afterwards.

Chapter 10

Office Boy

Life had been kind to me in many ways and fate took a hand when I was transferred from Accounts (they obviously thought I wouldn't make a good actor), to being Office Boy. This move probably saved me from dying of sheer boredom by giving me a great deal of freedom, inside and outside the works. Each morning, I collected the mail from the Lodge and took it to the Reception Room in the main office, sorted the letters and distributed them around the works. The journey was one of fascination for me because my travels would take me through all the workplaces where I had the opportunity to see men at their jobs.

First stop would be the Security Lodge. 'Morning, Mr Thomas.'

'Mornin, George,' would be the reply of the retired police sergeant who was always pacing up and down the room with hands clasped behind his back. The works Security was made up of Steel works employees who were too old or infirm to carry on working in their original jobs, and had been put in the Lodge as Security until retirement. Visitors to the works sometimes ignored the sleeping Lodgemen and went about their business without reporting in. After listening to a couple of stories I'd be on my way, passing a small office where former works' manager Tom Griffiths, had been put to await his retirement. The last of the old regime, Mr Griffiths, as Works Manager, would at one time sack a man for looking at him the wrong way. This quiet little man had ruled with an iron rod, but times had changed and he was gently demoted into an office with little to do all day other than stand on the office step watching workmen passing to and fro. I wonder what went through his mind as older workmen touched their caps to him as they walked past.

'Morning Mr Griffiths,' I'd say. A broad smile would be the response. I was rarely called upon to deliver mail to the man who had once commanded the highest post in the steel works.

I'd cross over the railway lines to the Electrical Department, situated on one side of a large two-storey brick building that also housed the General Stores and Archives. That was a fascinating discovery, like an ancient tomb. There were numerous racks of old Data, including documents listing properties and land owned by the steel works and bundles of handwritten letters by Lady Charlotte Guest, wife of the famous iron master John Guest. After spending time in the Archives I'd leave and deliver to the Structural Shop, Machine Shop and Carpenters' Shop, past the Wagon Repair Shop, the Smiths' Shop where two or three fires burned with bellows attached, the Pattern Shop and then across a roadway to the General Casting Foundry, a massive steel construction making ingot moulds and all types of castings.

On my first visit to the foundry I steeled myself before entering, expecting to see tired sweating bodies toiling away in the heat. I entered through the large doorway to see the inside showing decades of brown dust on walls, girders, light shades and just about everything else. I made my way through the foundry as smoke rose from one area and dust from another. There were the warning sounds of Claxton horns on overhead cranes, the constant noise of machinery and sparks flashed as white hot metal flowed from ladles into moulds. But where were the overworked sweating bodies? Where were the men tortured by excessive heat? Where were the foremen shouting abuse at the workmen?

Of course there weren't any. This was the twentieth century and the slavery of workmen in Welsh Steelworks had long ceased. Men slowly toiled at jobs while foremen walked about avoiding anything that might bring them into confrontation with union officials, who in turn looked for excuses to leave their work and head for a meeting with personnel.

The Iron and Steel Works at Dowlais became one of the best all round employers in the Merthyr valley. They were the glory days, but at that time staff workers were paid less than the general workforce. Staff workers were given small extras to kid them they were better off, such as free staff lunches. But you couldn't eat a bellyful of food then regurgitate it later for your family. At Christmas time a free staff dance was held at the City Hall Cardiff, food and drink supplied free of charge. Eventually this concession was withdrawn when, after one dance, senior staff workers had to be taken to hospital to have the alcohol pumped out of their stomachs.

After twelve months as office boy I was transferred to the Wages Department, a move that was to influence my whole future. The wages staff was made up of chief wages clerk Derlwyn Kent, wages clerk Tegwyn Phillips and comptometer operator, Christine Barry.

Derlwyn, in his forties was short in stature and wore glasses. His wife ran a small grocery shop from their home in Pant and Derlwyn also ran a small business selling sweets and cigarettes from the wages department at the Steel works. The chief wages clerk could be likened to Phil Silvers of Sergeant Bilko fame and he had a great influence on me. Every Monday morning, workmen's timecards were delivered to the wages department and we'd start to calculate the men's wages, working as quickly as possible to finish by Tuesday lunchtime when the desks were cleared, leaving some work about as camouflage. Then out came the playing cards.

'Right kids, are we ready? Brag today with a limit of sixpence.'

While the cards were dealt around the tables, Derlwyn smoked fags, Tegwyn smoked fags and I wanted to be grown up so I started smoking fags. Three fellows puffing away at cigarettes filled the office with smoke. Playing cards were dealt around the table and the amount of money won or lost was settled on payday. Suddenly, someone would break into song. 'We are two little lambs who have gone astray, Ba Ba Ba,' and we'd all join in the singing, a chorus of untrained voices until the door handle turned and the opening door wedged on the floor. We'd quickly put the playing cards in the drawer as accountant Wilf Price stumbled into the office. To avoid being caught red handed by someone opening the door and walking straight into the office, we had poured water onto the wooden floor blocks in front of the door to make them swell. The opening door wedged on the floor, giving us time to put the playing cards away and pretend we were working. When the person finally entered we'd start wiping the make believe sweat off our foreheads, grumbling that we didn't even have time to stop for a cup of tea.

Wilf Price would be annoyed. 'I've told you before Derlwyn, get that door fixed and, for goodness sake, keep the noise down.'

The chief wages clerk would look up. 'Sorry, Mr Price, we got carried away. It won't happen again.' Wilf Price would walk out of the room shaking his head.

The saying that you can't put an old head on young shoulders must have applied to me. I had no thought for 'tomorrow'. My only desire was to be at work all week for which I received my pay of two pounds fourteen and sixpence on a Friday that was handed to my mother. She gave me ten bob pocket money that I happily spent at the weekend. I didn't want to be a boxer, in the gym training or road running every morning. What I was doing was fine by me, but there was the constant niggling thought at the back of my mind of what I could be doing in the world of boxing.

In 1959, the year after I started work, two Welsh amateur boxers turned professional and were to become household names. Swansea's Brian Curvis entered the paid ranks along with Merthyr's Howard Winstone who fought his first pro fight beating Billy Graydon on points. Professional boxing had returned to Merthyr. Other amateur boxers also turned pro with Eddie Thomas who proved to be a top boxing trainer, and Merthyr became a hotbed of professional boxing. With local boys in the spotlight I envied the glory they received and all the money they were supposedly making. I had faded into obscurity since finishing training and boxing remained only in my mind.

My father is the third from left, standing (1935).

My sister Marilyn and me (1951)

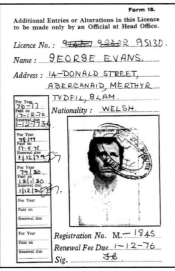

*My boxing managers licence,
obtained on 1st Sept, 1966*

My self supporting boxing ring.

*Redman Coleman.
Notorious fist fighter who
lived in China Merthyr*

*The boxing ring at my Troedyrhiw gym in 1974. Back row, left to right: Llew
Williams, my father; former boxer Gerald Jones; Joe Beckett; my younger
brother Wayne, and me.*

Eddie Thomas's Penydarren gym, the Old Lucania is the end building with first floor fronting.

Eddie with London promoter Jack Solomon celebrating Howard Winstones 29th birthday, April 17th 1968

Training time for Howard Winstone at Eddie's Penydarren gym. June 1967

In the Drill Hall Amateur boxing club. My father is sitting in the centre. I'm sitting in the centre on the floor. March 1951.

My grandfather, Morgan Evans in running pose in 1906.

Eddie Thomas in his boxing days – British Welterweight, 1949-51; Commonwealth 1951; European 1951.

Merthyr boxer Joe Fox and my father (on the right) sparring in 1934.

Dick Richardson,
European Heavyweight 1960-62

My father's boxing
licence, 12th June, 1933.

Joey Erskine (British Heavyweight 1956-58; Commonwealth 1957-58).
Benny Jacobs second on Erskine's right.

Jimmy Wilde

Tommy Farr, British Heavyweight
1937-38; Commonwealth 1937-38.

*Dai Dower, British Flyweight
1955-57; Commonwealth 1954-57;
European 1955.*

*My father and former Merthyr
pro boxer Billy O'Neill in 1971.*

*My father signing pro forms in the Merthyr Labour Club in 1933 with my
grandfather George Aris who managed him. My grandfather Morgan Evans
first standing on my father's right.*

Me sitting front row centre,
Army Cadets

With John Wall the night he won the
Welsh Lightweight Championship,
15 Feb, 1977.

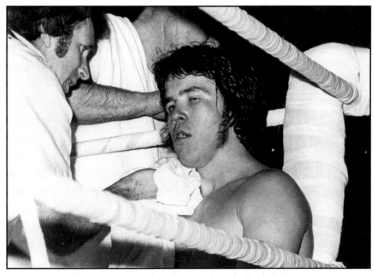

Cornering one of my boxers Gareth (Tashy) Jones

Freddie Welsh, British and World Lightweight Champion.

Me in my boxing pose, 1963.

Howard Winstone when he won the British Featherweight Champion on 2nd May, 1961. Lifting Winstone (on his right) is my father; behind him Eddie Thomas

John Wall, Welsh Lightweight Champion sitting between Joe Beckett and me at my Troedyrhiw gym in 1977.

Howard Winstone in front of Cefn Viaduct

Winstone Allen signing pro forms. I'm sitting on Allen's left Joe on his right at my Troedyrhiw gym, 11th August, 1981.

My father sitting in front of the fire at Troedyrhiw gym holding photo of Winstone.

The Angel Building, where I was introduced to boxing.

Hilary and me in Richards Arms.

Hilary and me, day we married, 18th April, 1960.

China. Rough area of Merthyr, no longer exists.

Merthyr Tydfil, looking north-west.

Office staff at Guest Keen

Georgetown, Merthyr

*Winning the Welsh Lightweight Championship at Marina Club, Penarth,
18th March, 1965. I'm wearing the dark (Welsh Champion) vest.*

*Paul Boyce and me during one of our Boxing Promotions.
Behind us is Ron Grey, Boxing Matchmaker*

Paul Boyce, Wynford Jones, President of ex-Welsh Boxers and me during the Howard Winstone Memorial Dinner at Rhydycar Leisure Centre, 2nd Feb, 2001.

In my promoting days at Patti Pavilion, February 1989.

Dowlais Steelworks – the heart of the town – c.1950

From left, Freddie Welsh, World Lightweight 1912-14, 1914-17; Tom Thomas, British Middleweight 1906-10, seated and Jim Driscol, European Featherweight 1912-13.

Jimmy Wilde, British Flyweight 1916-23; European 1914-15/1916-23; World 1916/1916-23.

Chapter 11

Hilary and the Bulfords

I was sixteen years old and going out on a Saturday night with my pals Michael, Clive and Baden. Dressed in our best suits we'd meet in Merthyr town, where, for four teenagers, seeing the electric street lights coupled with neon lighted pub signs, it might well have been Piccadilly. Mingling with other Saturday night revellers, young girls with their knee length skirts would get our admiring glances as we made our way to the Imperial Inn at the top end of town. We nervously entered the pub, looking around in case we were recognised before going into the back room, which, since we were under age we thought best. We sat looking around the dismally decorated room that had no other occupants and I reminded the others, 'Remember now boys, if we're asked we've just turned eighteen. Who's going for the drinks?'

'I'll go,' said Mike. He cautiously opened the door and glanced nervously up and down the corridor before quickly walking to the serving hatch, and returning shortly with a tray of drinks.

A couple of lagers later and feeling like men we made our way to the Palace Dance Hall which didn't sell alcohol, only soft drinks. As we joined the queue to pay to go in, one of the bouncers came across to me and said sternly, 'Oi, you can't go in the dance without a tie, butt.'

I pointed to my bootlace necktie.

'That's no good you've gotta have a proper tie,' said the bouncer who walked away and came back with a 'proper' tie. 'Give me a pound,' he said, 'and you can borrow this one. When you bring it back you can have your pound back.'

Jubilant once more we walked up the steps to the swing doors that led into the dance hall and looked in. Adjusting our eyes to the semi darkness we could see boys and girls dancing to the rhythm of a band, positioned on a stage at one end of the hall. Lights reflecting from a large glass ball rotating in the centre of the ceiling focused on everything and everybody, while around the walls boys were standing watching the girls dancing. We entered the dance hall and joined the army of boys and girls that were standing around the dance floor. We were mesmerised by the sight of dancing girls and slightly inebriated by the couple of beers we had drunk, but even more intoxicated by the lights and atmosphere.

A Saturday night at the dance and we had to get a couple of hours serious bird watching. After all, we couldn't dance so what choice did we have.

'Der, look at this one by ya boys,' said Clive as a smart blonde walked past. 'Wouldn't mind snogging 'er.' There was more chance of seeing a snowball in hell.

Nearing the end of the evening it was normal for two guys to start fighting over a girl and be thrown out of the dance to continue outside. When the fight ended, any black eyes received by the combatants were considered a badge of honour. Having witnessed the fights we'd begin our walk home. It took us through the centre of Merthyr, busy with Saturday nighters. At one shop a large mirror stood against the outside wall and suddenly one of us would become Harry Worth, standing by the mirror and moving an arm and leg up and down. Seeing the reflections made the others double up with laughter. We'd continue on our way to the bottom of town where, opposite the

Parish Church was a fish and chip shop, the aroma of which made us hungry and we'd wait to be served. On one occasion, Bernard, who worked in the shop, asked, 'How's it going then boys, did you manage to have a girl each tonight?'

We replied, 'Na, there were only tarts there anyway so we didn't bother.'

Bernard winked at another customer and asked, 'So what's wrong with a couple of tarts? I'll have to come with you one night to show you how it's done.'

'Nearly 'ad a fight though,' said Mike. 'Some bloke pushed into me and I asked him if he wanted to sort it, but I let 'im off.'

'Lucky for him then,' said Bernard winking at the customer again. Leaving the shop we began walking the last mile home eating our fish and chips.

One Saturday night after a couple of lagers we went to the Palace and again joined others standing around the dance floor. After I'd resigned myself to spending yet another night bird watching, two attractive girls danced past followed by the stares of all the boys. One of the girls, dark haired and brown eyed, slim and very attractive smiled at me (foolish girl), and I was struck by a thunderbolt. Shy with girls I might have been, regularly standing on the edge of the dance floor I might have been, but without giving a second thought I walked onto the dance floor, politely tapped the girl's shoulder and started dancing with the dark haired beauty as if I'd been dancing for years.

Okay, so maybe I did tread on her toes a couple of times, and perhaps I was tongue-tied but I did manage to ask her name.

'Hilary,' she said. 'Hilary Bulford.'

That night, the 2nd May, 1959 was Hilary's sixteenth birthday and her mother had allowed her to go dancing to Merthyr on a Saturday for the first time. (Poor soul.) We left the dance together and walked into Merthyr town centre where Hilary caught a bus home to Troedyrhiw, a large village three miles down the valley, where she lived with her parents. And so began my many bus journeys to Troedyrhiw. The fact that I'd only recently persuaded my parents to have a television on weekly hire made no difference. I'd arrive home from work and after rushing my meal I'd wash and change ready to catch a bus down the valley to meet Hilary. As I left the house my father would shout, 'We only had the TV for you and you're never in to watch it.'

Boxing? I didn't want to know. There were other things in life besides training every night. I wanted to be with the men drinking beer in pubs, going dancing and watching the pretty girls. But most of all I wanted to be with Hilary.

After a couple of weeks of us going out together Hilary invited me home to meet her parents. Wearing my best black suit, with three quarter length coat and velvet cuffs and collar, and drainpipe trousers, bought on the never-never, I journeyed by bus to Troedyrhiw. Leaving the bus at the square, I walked through the village certain that everyone admired me in my new suit. I passed a school, pubs, Ex-servicemen's club, went beneath a railway bridge and then past the small shopping centre to arrive at 2, Poplar Street. I knocked at the front door and was invited in by Hilary. The semi-detached house had two bedrooms, two downstairs rooms, a kitchen and bathroom added on. It was nicely furnished and well looked after. I was taken into the living room and introduced to Hilary's parents, Aaron and Bella Bulford. Aaron tapped the settee inviting me to sit next to him and I obliged, but politely refused the offer of tea. I was normally shy with strangers and this occasion was no different with Hilary's father making all the conversation.

'Are you working?' he asked.

'Yes.'

'Where?'

'Guest Keen steel works, in the wages office.'

There was a short silence then Aaron asked, 'Where do you live?'

'Clare Street, at the bottom of town.'

'So you're a boxer?'

'Yes,' I lied. More an ex-boxer but I didn't say as much. So my boasting to Hilary hadn't gone amiss.

'Not one for talking are you?' said Aaron, patting me on the arm.

When it was time for me to leave and say my goodbyes, I walked (on air) back to the square and caught a bus up the valley to Merthyr. My future jaunts around Troedyrhiw didn't go un-noticed as I strode through the village as if I owned the place.

At that time I didn't know about Aaron Bulford's violent behaviour after drink, the physical abuse and terror he meted out to his family, and the skivvying at home that Hilary was made to do.

Aaron Bulford, a small quiet man, was a native of Troedyrhiw. He had spent most of his working life in the pits, before leaving to work at Hoover where he stayed until his retirement. Being employed all those years in the dust riddled mines caused him considerable ill health. Added to this he smoked too many cigarettes and drank too much beer. Aaron had met and married Bella from Pentrebach, a small village on the side of the mountain just outside Merthyr. They eventually moved to live at 2, Poplar Street, Troedyrhiw, and that became the family home. Shortly before World War Two, Aaron, along with others had joined the Territorial Army. The idea was that each year while on two weeks' holiday from the pits they would join the TA's at an army camp and play soldiers. Each man would be paid two weeks' wages on top of holiday pay from the pits. Unfortunately, the year Aaron joined the TA's at camp World War Two started, and when the Territorial Army was called to defend the country Aaron was taken away to prepare for battle. Apart from a quick home visit leave, he spent the rest of the war years fighting in Europe.

Although he never discussed his wartime experiences with his immediate family, Aaron told me about some of his harrowing experiences as stretcher-bearer during battle. The horrific scenes that Aaron had witnessed were obviously distressing, and caused mental stress that stayed with him all his life.

As a stretcher bearer Aaron was required to rush to the aid of injured troops on the battlefield, seeing injured soldiers, some with limbs torn off and near to death. He also recalled entering a forest with his platoon and seeing the trees covered with dead bodies and bits of human limbs, the aftermath of bombing. Then, trapped by snipers, they had to dig trenches for cover and were unable to move for ten days, during which time they had to relieve themselves where they lay. When they tried to eat the smell made them vomit adding to the mess and stench. During darkness men crawled out of the trenches, poured petrol on dead bodies and burned them to alleviate the smell. After escaping from the trenches Aaron and his mates came upon an empty farm cottage that had been abandoned and they decided to spend the night there. Aaron's best friend went upstairs to sleep on the bed while the others remained downstairs. During the night an enemy tank fired a shell through the roof of the cottage killing Aaron's friend. When the war ended Aaron went home to his family in Troedyrhiw and returned to working in the pits.

Bella Bulford gave birth to seven girls, Mair, Val, Phyllis, Pat, Yvonne, Gwyneira, and Hilary. Bringing up seven daughters though could not have been easy, Val was reared from an early age by relations and Bella being mean and thrifty probably came from having to struggle to feed and clothe her family.

Aaron and Bella Bulford would regularly be in a Troedyrhiw pub, laughing and joking with their pals and singing a duet together. At stop tap they'd make their way home. The girls who were already upstairs in bed, listened to hear what sort of mood their father was in. Once inside 2, Poplar Street Aaron's mood changed and taking off his tie he'd throw it on the fire, then tip up the table and start smashing dishes. Bella would start shouting at him and he'd hit her as he carried on smashing the crockery and furniture. The end result was always the same, with Aaron getting all the girls out of bed in their nightclothes, and along with Bella being put outside onto the street in the early hours of the morning. Neighbours would appear on their doorsteps and curtains moved as preying eyes witnessed what went on. The police constable would be called and he'd say, 'Come on Mr Bulford let them back in.' But Aaron was adamant. 'No it's my house and they can stay out.' Bella and the girls then had to accept the offer of a bed for the night with their next-door neighbour Mrs Terrett.

All the girls were fearful of their father's violence towards them. There was never a happy mood at home for fear of upsetting Aaron and Bella. Outside 2 Poplar Street, Aaron Bulford was a quietly spoken man. The truth was that he ruled his family with a rod of iron, not one of the girls dared answer back for fear of being hit. He was a Jekyll and Hyde character, a bully who severely beat all the women in his household. Aaron's daughters grew up fearful of their father and only Val, reared by family relations whom she considered her real family, missed the beatings. But the quiet village of Troedyrhiw held a terrible secret that the majority of villagers didn't know existed; those that did kept the code of silence. Today, those villagers who knew would be scorned for not telling and saving the girls from being beaten. But until the end of the twentieth century domestic violence was considered acceptable; there was no safe haven then and divorce was considered out of the question for taking a beating from the spouse.

There is no doubt that his life experiences had made Aaron Bulford what he was. His mother died when he was young and he was reared by a violent father who beat him. He witnessed horrific war scenes as a stretcher-bearer; thousands must have suffered like him but there was no help then. Bella, despite being on the receiving end of Aaron's temper, always sided with him against their daughters. Although they gave their children a hard upbringing, Aaron and Bella always kept the girls clean, tidy and well fed. Hilary, the youngest, wore the hand-me-downs, something that was common in the valleys. Not many houses had bathrooms in those early days and Aaron would collect an empty wooden beer barrel from the local pub and cut it in half for the family to bathe in. With only two bedrooms in the family home, Aaron and Bella slept in one and all the girls in the other. I'm sure the following song was written for them.

'There were seven in a bed
And the little one said
Roll over, roll over
So they all rolled over
And one fell out
There were six in a bed . . . '

Hilary was the seventh and last-born to Bella and Aaron Bulford and became the skivvy. She had to clean the house from top to bottom and cook for the family. Though working in a local grocery store, Hilary was ordered to run home daily to cook dinner for two of her sisters, and if she was late she would often be reported to Aaron.

In time, five of the Bulford daughters were married and left Poplar Street, leaving only Hilary at home with her parents. As usual Aaron and Bella would go to the local pub on a Saturday night and at 'stop tap' invite drinking pals home, taking with them a crate of beer. Hilary, as a teenager would lie in bed hating the sound of drunken laughter coming from downstairs and longing for the day when she too could leave home. Poor Hilary regarded herself as a second-hand rose having to wear hand-me-downs, but being the seventh child she was different, having the class to look special in whatever she wore.

When Hilary became a teenager, she blossomed into an

attractive young lady. I became a young man who had met the girl of his dreams. Meeting in May meant we did our courting during spring and the summer months, spending time wandering up the mountains and witnessing the arrival of new mountain foliage. We listened to the twittering of birds courting and on a sunny day we'd look down into the village and watch the flow of cars, lorries and Corporation buses trundling along through the narrow dip beneath the railway bridge. Hilary and I 'cwtched' (hugged) each other as our gaze wandered up and down the valley. My thoughts were of love and a poem entitled, 'Troedyrhiw's Rose' was formed in my mind.

'From the honest dirt of Troedyrhiw
Seven bushes were planted and grew
From one bush sprouted a rose
The one that I was lucky and chose
The only rose that bloomed that way
Was Hilary born on the 2nd of May.'

This was Utopia, but little did we realise that it was to be short lived. Our dream world was to end quickly and we'd find ourselves having to cope with marriage and two young children while trying to survive on one small wage. There was to be no help from Hilary's family, and little help from my parents who had trouble enough coping with my two young brothers.

After we'd been courting for twelve months Hilary became pregnant and it was agreed by all that marriage was the best course.

Chapter 12

The Wedding and Family Life

On Easter Monday, April 18th, 1960, Hilary and I dressed in our best were married at Merthyr Tydfil register office. She was sixteen years old and I was seventeen. Two teenagers getting married and our only extravagance was a twenty-two carat Welsh gold wedding ring that used up all our savings. It was a glorious sunny day and families on both sides arrived wearing their Sunday best. Along with a number of guests we queued up in a corridor that reminded me of a dentist's waiting room when suddenly, a door opened and a woman appeared and asked us to go in. The office we went into was only big enough to accommodate Hilary and me, our parents, the best man, the registrar sitting behind a small desk and the woman who had called us in. The registrar, who had a serious look on his face quickly read words from a script and Hilary and I were told to reply when prompted. Then he looked up, gave a sigh and said, 'Right, that's it'.

We were married and then herded outside the building. It was all over and finished in about five minutes. But for two, happy, excited teenagers it didn't matter anyway. Although very young and naïve, there was never any doubt in our minds about getting married, and I, in particular, gave no thought to our nil finances.

After leaving the registry office, a couple of black and white wedding photographs were taken before we all clambered into cars for the dash down the valley to Troedyrhiw, where a reception was held. About twenty invited guests were eager to get to the wedding reception, not only to indulge in the free buffet but for the excuse to have a drink. Hilary's parents had arranged the reception at the Belle Vue Inn, Troedyrhiw, and everybody had a great time (I thought so anyway). We all squeezed into the small, side room where a buffet was laid out. Hilary looked attractive, while, in my opinion, all her sisters were second best as far as looks and personality were concerned.

The number of wedding presents we received wouldn't have filled a small sack. Aaron and Bella's wedding gift was to provide the small buffet and Billy and Maud gave us money to buy furniture. Hilary's sister Val, and her husband Trevor, though often absent on a day-to-day basis, always seemed to be present at functions organised by the Bulfords. But for Hilary and me it didn't matter. We didn't want or expect anything (oblivious to what others thought). We just wanted to live our lives together.

When we left the Belle Vue, for a day's outing to Cardiff by train, Hilary's father called her and said, 'Right, you've made your bed, you must now lie in it.' That was the last word on the subject. There was to be no help financially or otherwise from that quarter. I was too naive to realize what a burden I'd become to Hilary. After a lifetime of skivvying for her parents and some of her sisters in 2, Poplar Street, she was stuck with me at an age when I earned a pittance, had no savings, nothing of value to my name, nowhere to live and now, to boot, Hilary had been abandoned by her parents.

The woman friend my grandfather, George Aris, lived with offered to rent us the basement of her three-storied terraced house in the centre of Merthyr, and even though the council had condemned it as uninhabitable we accepted. The door to the basement flat opened into a dark, narrow passageway that led to a small kitchen, and from the kitchen was a bathroom used by the whole household. On one side of the stairs a door opened into the living room/bedroom and on the other side stairs led up to the first floor where my grandfather lived with his woman friend, her daughter and eventually her son-in-law. The whole basement reeked of damp. An open coal fire in the living room provided heat, and there was a gas cooker and electric lighting. We bought a bed settee and some bits of furniture, a second hand, black and white TV that didn't work very well (we could either watch the picture of only one station with no sound, or listen to the sound but no picture, the two wouldn't work at the same time), and a wireless on HP.

Washing machines, many supplied by the nearby Hoover factory provided housewives with modern washing facilities, but we couldn't afford one. Hilary, without complaint used an old-fashioned wood and brass scrubbing board. With an old stone bosh filled with hot water in which stood the scrubbing board, and a block of washing soap Hilary rubbed clothes clean with her bare hands, rinsed in cold water and then squeezed the excess water out before hanging them on the line to dry. The only direct access to the basement was along a back lane and through an archway between two small cottages, which led to a flagstoned back yard containing an outdoor toilet that we shared with the whole household.

That was our new home in the basement of 41, Union Terrace, and Hilary and I worked hard painting, decorating, scrubbing, cleaning and polishing until, eventually, years of dirt and decay disappeared. At last with our bits of furniture in place and sitting in front of a roaring coal fire, the flat looked comfy and we were happy. But we soon realized how difficult it was being married and living on small money.

Grandfather had his share of weaknesses, one of them being an eye for women. Having lost his true love, my grandmother, he still felt the need for a woman's company. He didn't ever attempt to remarry and was content with having a woman friend. Unfortunately, being timid, he was always domineered by the woman he lived with. Being weak willed, my grandfather allowed housekeeper, Mrs Roderick, to control the house at 65, Clare Street. When my mother and Connie married and left the family home George Aris was left alone with his housekeeper Mrs Roderick and they continually quarrelled. During the 1950's they decided to part company but being a coward in that respect, instead of asking the housekeeper to move elsewhere to live he moved out and went to live with my aunt Connie, leaving Mrs Roderick, whose own two daughters had also married and left home, living alone at 65, Clare Street.

But George Aris still had an eye for the women and he met lone mother, Gwen Owen, who had a three-storied house in Merthyr. They became friendly, and Grandfather, instead of living with Connie, was invited to move in with his lady friend. The saying, 'There is no fool like an old fool,' must have applied to my grandfather. A man of considerable means with his own home where his former housekeeper lived, he ended up lodging with a woman friend.

Grandfather was a man with sound business sense who, although he experienced sad times during his life, was always sharp of mind, until the unthinkable happened. While still only in his sixties he started suffering from senile dementia and was unable to hold a proper conversation or even know where he was. His woman friend arranged a marriage and they became man and wife.

After we'd been married a few months, Hilary gave birth to Deborah Lea, who came into the world with her mother's dark hair and pretty looks. With no help from her mother or sisters, Hilary had to find her own way to feed and look after a baby, change nappies and other general baby care. To try and make ends meet Hilary started work, and every morning wheeled baby Deborah in her pram three miles to Clare Street where my mother looked after her, until Hilary collected her after work. Eighteen months later Hilary gave birth to our second daughter,

Julie, who was also gifted with her mother's looks and Hilary was forced to give up work.

Being only eighteen years of age I was earning the small sum of four pounds seventeen shilling and six pence per week, when the average wage was twenty pounds plus. After paying the weekly rent of ten shillings, keeping a supply of coins for the gas and electric meters, making do with one bag of coal, and my bus fare to work there was a pitiful amount left for us all to live on. But Hilary was sensible, keeping me on the straight and narrow and an eye on our finances. My parents were helpful, but having little themselves there was not much to spare.

We were so busy trying to earn enough to live there was no thought of delving into obtaining handouts from the government, although just being employed then was enough to make us ineligible for help. It soon became apparent that when you're down it's extremely difficult to get help of any kind, from anywhere, but, being proud and not letting on about our true situation didn't help. Getting married at a young age and rearing two young daughters that were our pride and joy made us appreciate the simple things in life.

Professional boxing in Merthyr and Wales was on the up. Eddie Thomas, already managing many local boxers including the unbeaten professional Howard Winstone, signed other talented boxers from around the country. In 1960 the year of my marriage, Newport's Dick Richardson (Dick the milk) became European Heavyweight Champion. The larger than life fighter had a big following nationwide and it was during a contest against Brian London, at Porthcawl, that he hit the headlines controversially. The fight was stopped in the seventh round when Brian London sustained a cut eye and London's father, among others, complained bitterly. Richardson's trainer went across to London's corner to offer sympathy but London knocked him down. All hell broke lose with both camps fighting each other and fans throwing chairs into the ring. The result of that fracas was, the British Boxing Board of Control banning fathers from assisting in their son's corner. That same year outstanding Swansea boxer Brian Curvis, became British and Commonwealth Welterweight Champion.

The media focused on the highly talented Howard Winstone, who was trained by Eddie Thomas whose Penydarren gym was becoming well known in the boxing world.

I began to regret having stopped boxing when I could now have been earning. The other Merthyr boxers seemed to be 'in the money' and that was a commodity I sorely needed. But what fun times we had, dodging the manager of the grocery store when unable to pay the weekly bill and pretending not to be at home when the man called for the weekly payment for clothes bought on tick.

Many times on a Saturday night, to get out of Union Terrace we'd catch a bus to Hilary's parents at Troedyrhiw and watch television while Aaron and Bella went out for a drink. Hilary's father, because he was a former miner, was given a concession of free coal and one Saturday night while visiting I mentioned that we had no coal at home to light a fire. There was no offer of any, so once Aaron and Bella left for the pub I filled a carrier bag of coal from the full coalhouse. The following week I intended to do the same but Aaron, realising what I had done, had put a lock on the coalhouse door.

We were struggling to make ends meet and my father, who was already jobbing in his spare time, gave me chance to help him repair roofs, paint and decorate or whatever else needed doing to earn a few bob. We took a job painting for old Mrs Shipman, a Jew who lived in a big house in Merthyr. While we were painting she kept offering to sell us bits of old rag at sixpence each, 'To wipe up bits of paint', as she put it. But trying to get paid when the work was finished was like trying to get blood out of a stone and we finally had to accept that she owed us five pounds.

In my young eyes I had to start growing up. Thrust into the role of family man I wanted to follow other valley workmen to be accepted. And what did the normal working men do? They worked hard all week, and at the weekend spent a large slice of their wages on beer. Hilary, who'd been brought up in a working class environment and whose father played this scene, accepted the situation, and agreed to me spending some of our hard earned money this way.

Meanwhile I kept thinking about Merthyr fighters claiming glory in the pugilistic arena, and the supposedly big money they were earning at boxing. I began to regret having finished with the game.

The year was 1961 and unbeaten Howard Winstone was matched against unbeaten Terry Spinks for the British Featherweight Title. Winstone asked my father if he would be in the corner with him on the most important fight of his career so far, and use his skills to massage him in preparation for all his future contests. My father's services as a masseur were widely recognized, and he treated people with muscular problems and was in great demand to assist fighters.

Howard Winstone stopped Terry Spinks and became the new British Featherweight Champion. The worldwide media was attracted to Merthyr. Winstone stayed champion for an incredible eight years and went on to win the European, Commonwealth and eventually the World Championship.

Thanks to amateur trainer Billy Evans who reintroduced boxing to Merthyr during the 1950's, the extraordinary talents of boxer Howard Winstone and the training of Eddie Thomas, boxing in Merthyr had been revived.

Chapter 13

From Union Terrace and into Boxing

Two years living in a cellar, managing on small money and rearing two young children, yet life wasn't all that bad despite our predicament. Most would have found the position daunting but we had our own little family and a dream. We had a dream that one-day we'd have our own home. We had a dream that one-day we'd earn enough to live without going into weekly debt. We had a dream that one-day we'd be able to look out of the window without seeing brick walls in front of us. Part of our dream came true in 1963 when my mother called to say there was a small cottage for sale in the mining village of Abercanaid, on the border of Merthyr town, and the asking price was five hundred pounds. Despite not having a penny saved we made enquiries and were hopeful that Merthyr Council would lend us the money. But we were told we'd need two hundred pounds deposit. Where were we going to get two hundred pounds?

The answer to that question came from my mother and father who gave us the deposit, probably all of their savings, and we arranged a mortgage from Merthyr Council for the rest to be paid back at four pounds a month. We couldn't believe our luck. At last we could move from the confined cellar flat to the village of Abercanaid, built at the foot of a mountain, on the far side of the river and two miles from Merthyr. Having only one main access road for transport meant Abercanaid was fairly secluded.

At one time the demise of mining had left much unemployment in the area, but the development of the Hoover washing machine factory nearby provided new work, thus revitalizing and bringing prosperity to Merthyr and the surrounding community.

Our new home at 4, Catherine Square, on the approach to Abercanaid, was an old, terraced, stone cottage with two rooms upstairs, two rooms downstairs, no bathroom and a toilet with no water supply at the bottom of a long garden. There was no rear access to the cottage and the front door opened onto a footpath that ran the whole length of the terrace. The Squares, regarded by some as the poorest part of Abercanaid, had to accept the view of the Hoover factory built on the far side of the river, but benefitted from a close community spirit that had long been absent further down the village. Our two young daughters Deborah and Julie enjoyed the freedom of their new environment, and were no longer restricted to a small square yard for their only play area. They attended the village school, enjoying the company of other children and the freedom of being able to play in the surrounding fields. The lack of traffic congestion provided relief for the parents.

Eventually Merthyr Council supplied running water to our outdoor toilet, the first in the Squares to have a flush toilet but still at the end of the garden. There was no more carrying buckets of water whenever we wanted to go to the loo. Unfortunately a footpath ran past the toilet and the sound of someone passing meant the toilet occupant remained quiet until the footsteps faded!

Then we began to think about having a bathroom. It was a toss up between buying a secondhand washing machine (Hilary must have been one of the last people having to use a scrubbing board) or a steel bath fitted into a two-foot wide partitioned space at one end of our small kitchen. Whatever we chose would have to be paid for weekly. The choice was a bathroom, so small we could only get into the bath at one end. We were the talk of the place, the first to have a 'real bathroom' in the Squares! The Hilton Hotel, the Ritz? We didn't have to go that far. This was our five star hotel and we loved every bit of it. We also had our own garden where I grew vegetables, but not flowers that looked nice but couldn't be eaten.

The next few years were happy for us all but it was still a struggle. Each week I dug coal out of the tips on the mountainside but it was mostly slag and burnt quickly. During cold weather I had to carry a bag of coal down the mountain every day. I'd spend the day at the steel works while Hilary worked in a local factory. Then in the evening, I'd meet my father and work at painting in 'Thomas' pies' Merthyr factory.

Boxing was constantly on my mind as a means of earning money. Of course I was naïve, not fully realizing how much hard work and effort would have to be put into training. I didn't realize that the boxing business thrives on the hard work and honesty of fighters, trainers, and the many involved in the game for little reward. Neither did I realize that boxing was tainted with some dishonest boxing managers, promoters and others wanting to make money on the backs of trusting fighters. Once, while visiting my parents I saw my father in conversation with Merthyr middleweight boxer John Gamble, formerly managed by Eddie Thomas, who had matched him with middleweight knockout specialist Teddy Haines. The result was that Gamble was knocked out and taken to hospital, and the British Boxing Board of Control then decided to take away his boxer's licence.

Gamble chose to make a comeback, asked my father to train him and I was invited to join them, thus taking me back into boxing. I was now twenty years old and I realised that after five years out of boxing it was going to be extremely difficult to start again. I didn't have the same interest in boxing as my father, but for me there was the need to earn some extra money. John

Gamble and I were joined by Stan Thomas of Peters Pies and TBI airports fame.

Former amateur boxer Terry Andrews offered us the use of his boxing gym in a hall beneath the old cinema in the mining village of Aberfan where, previously, dances had been held on Friday nights. Training with Gamble, a seasoned pro who knew the fight game, was ideal because we sparred together and I learned a lot of techniques. Because Gamble had a car we were able to visit other gyms for sparring, and the sound of the Searchers singing chart-topper 'Needles and Pins' blasted out from the car radio as we travelled. With my father as trainer it couldn't have been better.

After six months training at Aberfan, the end of 1963 was approaching when my father rented the Welfare Hut in Plymouth Street, Merthyr, starting his own gym two nights a week and bringing amateur boxing back to Merthyr. Eddie Thomas had a boxing gym at Penydarren but was mainly for the use of professional boxers and top amateurs looking to turn pro.

Fathers brought their young sons to the new boxing club thinking back to Merthyr's famous boxing era.

Dick Owen brought his young sons to the gym to be shown the rudiments of boxing. One of them, Johnny, went on to become British, European and Commonwealth bantamweight champion. While the Owen lads trained, their father Dick watched.

The Plymouth Street gym was packed with all sorts wanting to learn how to box. There were rich kids and there were poor kids all with dreams of becoming a champion boxer. Many fathers pushed their reluctant sons into boxing and stood around watching them, subconsciously seeking glory through them.

Gym nights would see a hall full of young would-be boxers trying to skip and dodge those working on punch bags. Others would be shadow boxing or sparring, trying not to step on those doing floor exercises. A number of small lads were sent to the gym so that their mothers could have a break, but they just ran around being a flaming nuisance. Having read about local boy hero Howard Winstone making good, young boys dreamed about the glory of becoming a champion and the wealth that was supposed to go with it. But for the majority of the lads and their fathers the dream would not become a reality.

Boxing is a hard, competitive sport and to succeed one has to really want to do it, whether for glory, financial gain or both. The demand on an individual boxer is such that he needs to be strong, tough and fit, train twice a day, spar regularly and be prepared to travel and set aside the life of drinking and socialising for long periods at a time. To be good at the fight game a boxer needs to make it an obsession and achieve 90% fitness and stamina. Maybe then, if he's lucky enough to have 10% determination, heart, talent and the special ingredient, plus 'luck' he'll became a champion. For me, it was hard but the need was there. I wanted the recognition and acknowledgment of being at least good at the sport. But most of all I needed the money to improve the quality of life for my family.

Months of hard work followed as I tried to knock my body into shape. Although lean and fit looking my body wasn't used to rigorous exercise and strenuous use. I did early morning running and trained in the gym three and four nights a week. I carried an axe up the mountain for tree chopping at weekends and then carried the logs home for firewood. I made two lead weights to carry when doing road-work and using the same weights in a standing position I punched into the air continuously for long periods to strengthen my arms. I dug the garden non-stop and when finished I'd started digging it all over again. Office work suited me because I could save all my physical energy for training.

For my first amateur fight on returning to boxing I entered the Welsh Championships in 1964 along with stable-mate, Stan Thomas who was later declared unwell by the doctor and was unable to box. I was drawn against the previous year's champion and lost on points. Some months later we boxed a return match and I reversed the decision. A fight had been arranged for me locally against an opponent from St Athan and I was fit, confident and looking forward to getting another win under my belt. My father had always told me not to lose my head and get involved in 'mixing it', but to use my skills and box. Had I done as I was told I would have achieved more in the game. Instead, I waded in and traded punches with my opponent and cracking my eyebrow against his head. I felt a terrific pain across my eye and as the blood started to pour down my face the referee stopped the contest. What an idiot I was, why didn't I listen to my father? Not only did I lose the fight by being stopped but the cut was so bad that it needed stitching. A week later, the stitches were removed but it was weeks before the cut healed enough for me to spar again. Then I pestered my father to arrange a return with the boxer from St Athan. I wanted revenge and to put the record straight. After what seemed like ages a rematch was fixed. My opponent was confident having already stopped me once but I was determined to prove myself the better, and this time I boxed as I knew how. The ref stopped the fight in the third round to save my opponent from taking further punishment.

It wasn't long before the Welsh Championships came around again and I entered for the second time, winning two fights in the quarter and semi finals at the Maindy Hall Cardiff to challenge for the Welsh Finals at Penarth a week later. I completely out-boxed my opponent and became Welsh Lightweight Champion of 1965.

Then, suddenly I was promoted to wages clerk at Dowlais Steel Works. What a dilemma. I was still not earning good money but it was security and with a family I needed that. My training would have to be fitted in around my day job and many times, carrying a bag of clothes I'd run the three miles uphill to the steel works where I'd shower, change into my suit and be in the office by starting time. Believe you me, it was bloody hard, but I'd had a taste of top amateur boxing by this time and I appreciated the back handers, and a little bit of glory.

Because I was Welsh champion the offers to turn pro were being put to me by boxing managers. But as an amateur I was given a prize plus expenses and that seemed very reasonable to me so I decided to stay that way.

A succession of amateur fights followed. I lost a few but won most and quickly put myself among the top amateur boxers. My father was keeping a watchful eye on my progress and he trained me as he had top boxers before me.

While training at Plymouth Street, John Gamble decided to make a move regarding his own boxing career by asking Cardiff's Benny Jacobs to manage him.

Gamble, my father and I travelled to Cardiff to meet Jacobs who had a boxing gym above part of the old fruit market in Custom House Street. Although as fly as a bag full of monkeys, Benny was a likeable man, short and thickset with a sense of humour and a great knowledge of the boxing world. Benny's gym had the look and atmosphere of real boxing with a floor ring, punch bags, boxing posters pinned to the walls and an old weigh-in scale. There was the smell of dust and wintergreen oil and worn paintwork on walls where people had leaned while watching the boxers training. I was introduced to other pro boxers who were known in the boxing world and were regularly in the public eye, and I discussed with them the rudiments of pro boxing and liked the welcoming signs. Eventually we left Benny's gym and headed for home, past the notorious Bute Street where in the evening young tarts sold their bodies to boost their bank balances. The following day the same girls became ladies working in an office, pronouncing their Hs and giving disgusted looks to anyone vulgar enough to mention sex. At the end of St Mary Street we drove past Cardiff Castle, joined the A470 and headed for Merthyr. Gamble's application for a new boxing licence was turned down by the British Boxing Board of Control, and so Benny Jacobs, who had a lot of connections, advised him to go to Australia where there was no board of control and he wouldn't need a licence to box.

Meanwhile my father built up the Merthyr ABC and amateur boxing once again flourished in Merthyr. Amateur Boxing Association rules state that an amateur club is only allowed one official trainer and at Merthyr ABC that was Billy Evans. At the same time, a boxing club could have as many assistant trainers as they wished. Due to the high rent paid at Plymouth Street it was decided to find premises elsewhere and in 1967 the Merthyr Labour Club agreed to rent us the old concert hall once again.

As Welsh Champion, I represented Wales a number of times, and on one occasion was asked to represent North Wales against Holland in a show to be held in Rotterdam. This was because North Wales Amateur boxing representatives planned to enrol boxers from outside their region in an effort to win a match between the two countries and win the cup that had eluded them for so long.

I arranged time off work, bought new boxing gear (that I couldn't really afford) and suffered the discomfort of having to travel from South to North Wales in the backspace of a two-seater car. The other two occupants enjoyed the comfort of seats while I, being the last to be picked up was given Hobson's choice! We eventually arrived five hours later and I had become so cramped up that I needed help to get out of the car. I met the North Wales team secretary who promised me 'ample expenses' to cover costs. We stayed the night in Bethesda, and the following morning we joined the other boxers and about 20 officials and their wives, driven by coach to Liverpool and boarded an aeroplane for Holland. Thrilled to bits I was, my first flight on an aeroplane and, I thought about to stay in some fine hotel. Well, not quite, the guesthouse was tidy enough but all the boxers slept in the same room! Unfortunately, I had to share a bed with a member of the team who kept farting all night! The following morning I was asked to join the rest of the team to go running. Running the same morning as the fight? No way, I didn't bother and let them carry on without me.

We were shown the sights of Rotterdam before travelling to the stadium. There I was immediately put under pressure when told that I was first on the bill, with the expectation that I would win and boost morale among my fellow Welshmen. Oh hell! What a responsibility. Still I'd been recruited for that purpose so I suppose it was up to me.

In the dressing room, busy with newspaper reporters and officials darting about trying to look important, the Welsh team, having weighed and been examined by the doctor, changed into their boxing gear. The boxers were each given a small Welsh badge and told to follow the team manager out into a huge hall where the boxing was to be held. The Welsh team climbed into the boxing ring and stood against the ropes on one side while the Dutch team lined up on the other side. Starting with the lightest weight first, the boxers were announced and each walked into the ring centre where he handed his opponent a Welsh badge and in return received a wooden table lamp in the form of a windmill from their Dutch opponent. Okay, so far so good. The two boxing teams then returned to the dressing room leaving my opponent and me in the ring to contest the first bout. The MC announced the contest to polite applause from the spectators and the contest began. A good, fast, three rounds of boxing followed and at the end I won my contest by beating the Dutch champion on points. That year, the North Wales team won the much sought after trophy, but unfortunately I never did receive my promised expenses for whatever reason from the North Wales officials.

During the four years I boxed as an amateur, constantly at the back of my mind was the thought of turning pro and earning money. I'd always considered professional boxers to be the cream of boxing and secretly hoped that one day I'd be good enough to become one. So, I started making enquiries in the world of professional boxing to discover what sort of money the boxers were paid. But getting information out of boxers was extremely difficult, and few wanted others to know how much they were being paid to box. I discovered that many pro boxers were actually paid very little, and I began to suspect that certain boxing managers were not disclosing to their fighters how much they would be paid before a contest. If fighters asked those particular managers how much they'd get they were kept in the dark and told to concentrate on the training and not worry about money.

According to the British Boxing Board of Control, a boxer's purse money must be agreed before a contest and collected from the promoter by the manager after the fight. The manager then deducted expenses from the purse money and 25% of the remaining amount would be the manager's fee.

But it was clear that some Welsh managers cocked their noses at the Boxing Board by not disclosing to their boxers how much they were earning. After the fight the managers in question would hand the boxer a few pounds and expect him to accept without question. The boxers were never shown a contract. The Boxing Board's rules state that a manager's signature alone is sufficient on a contract.

Exploitation of boxers was more widespread before the 1980's when travel and communication were not so easy and most boxers looked towards being managed locally. But the time when a boxing manager was considered total boss and the fighter an illiterate bum was coming to an end. Most boxers were getting wise. Unfortunately, my impression was that some of the new managers who came on the boxing scene would have whispered in their ears, 'Keep the fighter in the dark, the less he knows the better'.

Professional boxers are proud men, and rather than admit getting tucked up by their managers will put on an act. They live the high life of fine clothes, flash cars and nice houses. The truth is that most, apart from the lucky ones, have their clothes on the never never, cars on hire purchase and buy their houses with a big mortgage. All this encouraged by those managers who were happy to give the impression they were looking after a fighter.

I was sitting at home thinking about boxing, 'Should I turn pro, shouldn't I turn pro?', when it was all decided for me. The WABA had chosen someone who was not as good as I was to represent Wales in an international boxing contest. My mind was made up for me. I was going to turn professional.

Chapter 14

Boxing Pro

The two top boxing managers operating in South Wales during the sixties were, colourful Benny Jacobs, whom I met during my visits to his gym in Custom House Street, and Merthyr's Eddie Thomas. Most of Benny's fighters spoke well of the man who had made his name in boxing by managing British Heavyweight Champion Joey Erskine and many other boxers. The Cardiff manager, devious and cunning, convinced two of his fighters, Harry Carroll and Lenny (the Lion) Williams that they could win the British Featherweight Title off Merthyr's formidable Howard Winstone. Benny was content with having a good payday, while both of his fighters had to suffer being battered to a stoppage defeat by Winstone's magical fists.

Opposite Benny's gym was the 'Ringside' nightclub that he owned and where, having invited us, he would spill yarns about some of his colourful patrons. But, Benny sailed close to the wind and was under police scrutiny. The boxing manager and nightclub owner was renowned as a big gambler and at one time was banned from every horserace course in the country. But this didn't stop Benny from devising a 'get rich quick scheme' at the bookies' expense by tapping telephone wires from the racecourses to the bookies.

After heavyweight boxer Joey Erskine retired, he claimed that Benny had taken a fee for him to throw a fight against heavyweight prospect Billy Walker. But, despite Benny's brush with the law, he must have provided something of substance for his fighters because most stayed loyal to him.

The other top boxing manager in Wales was Eddie Thomas from Merthyr. The former British, Commonwealth and European boxing champion was the more recent past hero from the boxing town. Eddie, who had put on weight since his boxing days was tall and well built. People were happy to be in the company of a man who had plenty of personality, seemed to be well liked and managed champions Howard Winstone and Eddie Avoth, future champion Ken Buchanan and other top boxers. Constantly in the limelight, Eddie, who enjoyed being in the public eye, was a good trainer who spoke about boxing with authority and his boxers accepted with confidence what he said. The boys Eddie trained were at ease, knowing that he had been through the training routines himself and understood how a pro boxer should train. Many Merthyr boxers that I once trained with in my father's gym had signed with Eddie, and many a time I'd watched them with envy working out at the Penydarren gym.

I decided to visit Eddie's boxing gym at Penydarren, on the outskirts of Merthyr. The former Billiards Hall was a large, dirty, dilapidated building, the ground floor of which consisted of empty shop premises and on the first floor was the former snooker hall converted into a gym. I climbed the creaking stairs to the top, turned left through a door into the gym where, in a boxing ring, Howard Winstone was sparring with Terry Crimmins, a Cardiff lad managed by Benny Jacobs, who was sitting by a large window that stretched the whole length of the room. I watched as Winstone lay into his sparring partner, and wondered if Crimmins was being paid enough to warrant the punishment he had to take as Winstone's left jab kept prodding relentlessly into the Cardiff boxer's face.

I looked around the large room where two boxers punched bags hanging from the ceiling while others skipped on the wooden floor. I walked across the gym to a small dressing room, of similar appearance to the rest of the building. There was no sign of Eddie Thomas, and while helper Roy Sears timed boys training he handed someone two empty bottles and asked him to nip down to the road to a pub for some water. There were no showers or washing facilities in the gym, and at this particular time there was no water supply.

Of all the South Wales valley fighters that Eddie had once managed and who trained at his Penydarren gym, only Howard Winstone was still boxing. I wondered about the condition of the gym, but realized that many good fighters had trained there, and if it was good enough for them it was certainly good enough for me.

At first, asking Eddie Thomas to manage me seemed the obvious choice as I was living in Merthyr. Eddie knew a lot about the fight game and appeared to look after his fighters. Knowing all the Merthyr boxers that Eddie had managed, I discussed with some of them the possibility of asking Eddie to manage me but I discovered that all was not what it seemed. The fighters I spoke to didn't box as often as they would have liked and when they did fight, the money eventually paid to them by Eddie was a lot less than they had expected. On some occasions, certain boxers didn't get paid at all. Most young boxers came from poor backgrounds and initially the thrusting of a few pounds into their hands made them feel like paupers discovering gold. It appeared that the main purpose for many of Eddie's boxers was to provide unpaid sparring for Winstone and to make up the bill on shows promoted by Eddie, London boxing promoter Jack Solomons or Les Roberts, matchmaker of the National Sporting Club. It became apparent to me after making enquiries, that some of Eddie's fighters, fed up with those conditions, were considering being managed by someone else. But rather than confronting Eddie and asking for their contracts back, those fighters stopped boxing altogether.

Boxers managed by Eddie Thomas were overawed by his reputation, mesmerized by him and afraid to confront him to discuss the problems. Knowing Eddie, I well understood the situation. He had a commanding manner that was difficult to oppose. The old adage that top boxers rarely make good managers must have applied to Eddie Thomas. I discovered that although Eddie was a good boxing trainer, his managerial abilities were limited. Eddie was in contact with people in London who, on discovering the phenomenal talent of Howard Winstone, swooped on Merthyr Tydfil, smelling rich pickings that were easy to plunder because Eddie Thomas willingly allowed top boxing people to manipulate him.

What a dilemma for me. Here I was an ordinary fighter just wanting to earn and I thought hard about the situation. For me it was mainly the money. The glory would be nice and if any came along it would be appreciated. One big difference I had noticed was that the Merthyr boxers were better trained than the Cardiff ones. So, with my father training me in Merthyr Tydfil, I decided to look towards Cardiff for a manager.

The man I eventually chose to manage me was Cardiff's Mac Williams, who was new to pro boxing. He didn't have the same connections as Benny Jacobs but was young, keen and ambitious. Not having a champion in his stable, Mac worked hard trying to achieve that goal. Reading about Mac in the newspapers, I realised he was a big man who liked attention, had a flamboyant style and turned out to be like most other Cardiffians, a good talker. After a conversation with Mac it was wise to check the coins in your pocket to make sure the heads were still on them. Although he lived in Cardiff, the new boxing manager proudly claimed to have been born somewhere near Merthyr. Mac travelled to Merthyr to meet my father and me, and after that meeting I signed a three-year contract. Then started years of hard graft which included early morning running and gym' work. Soon after I turned pro with Mac, stable mate Dai Harris joined me and also turned pro with him. Supervised by my father, we trained and sparred together along with other Merthyr boxers at the Merthyr Labour Club. We were regarded by some as renegade Merthyr boxers who'd signed with someone other than Eddie Thomas. Dai and I regularly travelled to Mac's gym where we sparred with Cardiff boxers. Also, back in our Merthyr gym we sparred hundreds of rounds, knocking lumps out of each other.

I was determined to do well in professional boxing and knew that to succeed I had to be tough, strong and durable. I had a good chin, never having been knocked off my feet, but I reckoned without the problem of my eyebrows cutting and preventing me from earning big money. Being cut during every fight meant that after a contest I was unable to box again until the cuts had healed. But the incentive to earn money still drove me on.

Being managed by a Cardiff man meant that I had to travel to Cardiff regularly, on many occasions accompanied by Hilary and my young daughters, Deborah and Julie who would stay with Mac's wife until I'd finished training. My father's advice always rang in my ears, 'To be a good pro boxer you need to live boxing'. But I was working full time in a good steady job. With a family to support I needed the security and so boxing would always have to come second.

Is boxing a hard sport? Of course it is; only a fool or a liar will say it's not. It's true that a body will get used to taking punishment to a certain extent and cope better, but getting hit still hurts. But, the fighting is only part of it. The rest is having to devote one's life to the sport and living the life of an athlete to keep the body toned. It also means leaving the comfort of your home to spend the evening in the gym and travelling to shows. Yes, it is a hard sport.

The only way I could manage all the training was because I had an understanding wife, looking after two children alone while I was training and travelling away boxing. It couldn't have been easy for her. Life wasn't ideal for either of us and we had our rows, but all in all we strove forward together.

As an amateur I'd always trained hard, but as a professional there was a need to increase my training. A couple of weeks before a fight I'd get up at about five thirty in the morning and if it was bitterly cold, look out of the kitchen window and ask myself if missing one morning's run would matter. Then, convincing myself otherwise, I'd open the cottage door and step out onto the tarmac footpath, quickly closing the door behind me to keep the cold out. Dressed in an old pair of trousers, T-shirt under a woollen jumper, woollen hat on my head and hobnailed boots on my feet I'd begin slowly jogging uphill towards the mountain. It would be beginning to get light as I reached the dirt road that snaked up the mountain and I'd curse myself for forgetting gloves. I would feel the cold enter my lungs as I worked my body harder to climb uphill and reaching a flat part of mountain, I prepared myself before climbing to the top of a shale tip. It was cold and I couldn't get warm never mind how hard I ran; sweat oozed through my skin, drying cold instantly. Bracing myself for the imminent graft I'd take a deep breath and start to run giving little hops until I reached the top of the tip where I'd lean forward with hands on my knees gasping for breath. It would be easy running down the other side but my legs would shake, having been forced to climb the slope, they were now rebelling. But it was a chance to get my breath back before continuing along the mountainside towards Colliers' Row, and then down the dirt road to the foot of the mountain. A short run that morning, just thirty minutes, but enough because after spending the day at Dowlais steel works I'd be sparring in the evening. Reaching a stream that cascaded down the mountainside I'd jump across, turn and follow the route where the old canal once ran. Seeing my cottage I'd quicken my pace and tramp the tarmac footpath, not realizing the noise would probably wake neighbours. On arriving at the cottage, I'd enter to see Hilary lighting a coal fire to warm the house for Deborah and Julie to wake and come downstairs and get ready for school. Another run completed and I'd feel good, another feather in my cap. I'd wipe myself dry (no shower), change into my suit, drink a cup of tea and hurry to catch the bus to work.

Chapter 15

First Professional Fight

My first professional fight was arranged against a tough black fighter called Junior Lindo, at the Colston Hall, Bristol, on the 26th September, 1966. I was looking forward to becoming a paid fighter. My natural weight was around nine stone ten pounds, but it was assumed that fighting at a lighter weight was to my advantage. The couple of days before the fight were torture. At that time, the harmful effects of dehydration weren't generally known and many boxers made the error of losing too much weight before a contest, not realising that all the effort was weakening them to the point of being dangerous.

On the morning of the fight my father and I travelled to Cardiff where we met Mac and went on to Bristol. We arrived at the Colston Hall for the one o'clock weigh-in but there was no sign of my opponent. I weighed in at nine stone two pounds, was examined by the doctor and taken to a restaurant for a meal before going back to the Colston Hall, where I found an easy chair to rest for the afternoon. Evening soon came around and I was beginning to wonder if Junior Lindo was going to turn up at all when a black fellow walked into the hall and I realised that my opponent had arrived. Junior Lindo weighed-in at one stone heavier than me and Mac Williams asked my father what he thought about the extra weight.

'George will beat him,' was his reply.

'Alright with me,' I said, trying to sound unimpressed.

We found the dressing room and secured a space by one of the walls. Three other boxers, assisted by their handlers, were changing. They each claimed wall space that soon became littered with strips of plaster cut into lengths, ready to wrap around the fighters' knuckles. I changed into my boxing gear and Mac bandaged my hands before putting tape around each fist. Then, I sat and waited until it was my turn to box. My thoughts were on my forthcoming fight. I was nervous; there was no denying it. After four years of boxing in the amateurs as a senior, what I'd hoped for had finally happened. I'd turned pro, able to earn. After my first fight I'd be initiated into the realms of professional boxing. Everything about professional boxing seemed different. Men who were paid for what they were doing seemed to do it that little bit better. I was so full of my own thoughts I hardly noticed Mac and my father busying about preparing for when I would be called to box. The dressing room door opened and a smartly dressed boy carrying a new hold-all appeared. He sauntered across the room and claimed a chair before being joined by his manager. 'I'm first on the bill,' he told everyone. 'Feel good tonight, should end it quick like.' The other fighters smiled and I thought he must be a good fighter to think that way, while I had butterflies going non-stop in my stomach. The boastful boxer stripped to reveal a tanned, muscular body. He changed into new gear, taped and gloved before shadow boxing around the dressing room until the whip called him to box. He gave everyone a confident wink and left.

I was second on the bill and my father rubbed Vaseline over my body to stop abrasions, then I put my dressing gown on and waited to be called. Suddenly, the boxer who'd left only minutes earlier was being helped back into the dressing room, apparently he'd been knocked out. I thought, 'Oh boy, and he was so confident.'

The whip called me and while my father grabbed my towel, Mac, carrying his bag of corner gear, followed me into the hall full of cheering spectators. I climbed through the ropes into the boxing ring and scraped my boots in a tray of resin to help prevent slipping. The MC climbed through the ropes and started announcing the contest. 'My Lords, Ladies and Gentlemen. The second bout of the evening is a featherweight contest over six, three minute rounds between, in the blue corner from Merthyr Tydfil, in South Wales, George Evans.' There was clapping and cheering from spectators. 'And in the red corner from Manchester, Junior Lindo.' Another round of applause erupted. The MC left the ring and the referee climbed in, walked to the centre and called Lindo and me to join him to be reminded of the rules. 'Right boys, I want a clean fight, no butting, no holding. If I say "break" then you must step back. If one man is knocked down then his opponent will go to a neutral corner until I tell him to box on. Is that clear?' Lindo and I nodded in agreement and the ref said, 'Right, go back to your corners and come out fighting.'

Although a little apprehensive, I felt confident. Mac and my father, knowing of my liking for 'mixing it' kept telling me to box, not to get involved in a brawl that could lead to me getting cut.

The timekeeper shouted, 'Seconds out, first round,' and the bell sounded. My opponent had come to fight and he waded in punching with two hands, but I jabbed him and moved away. Lindo wanted to make a fight of it and tried to force the pace but I boxed, jolting him with jabs and following with right crosses. I boxed in that fight the way I should have boxed in all my fights, no brawls, just boxing as I knew how and I won every round to win the fight on points.

Small hall boxing shows were a regular feature of entertainment. The halls were normally full of spectators with bookies' runners darting up and down the aisles taking bets. After three or four preliminary bouts the top of the bill fighters would enter the hall to the sound of 'March of the Toreadors' and the crowd cheering. The fighters would climb into the ring and scrape their boots in resin while one of the cornermen took their dressing gowns. The MC would enter the ring and start introducing all the champions and well-known fighters who were in the hall, who in turn would jump into the ring, wave to the crowd and wish the fighters luck. Then the MC would introduce the two fighters topping the bill. The hall was a place of excitement as the fighters both fought their best and when the fight ended there would be the usual cheering and jeering while bookies' runners handed out money to those who'd bet the winner. Newspaper reporters, given a table against the ringside would be shouting into bakerlight telephones while trying to unravel the phone lead that always got caught in table legs. This was boxing at its best.

Many a time while waiting for a bus to go to Mac Williams's Cardiff gym I'd ask myself if it was worth all the hard work. Was it worth leaving the comfort of my home, my wife and two young daughters of whom I saw little before a fight. As usual I'd board the bus for the drive down the old A40 that would eventually take me to the City, down City Road to Shakespeare Street where I'd leave the bus and walk to the old building where Mac's fighters trained.

Shortly after my first pro fight I entered Mac's gym to see a couple of boxers training. Mac saw me and shouted, 'Hi George, how's it going?' The others nodded. Mac 'the voice', without waiting for me to reply said, 'Right George, get stripped off and onto the scale, let's see what you weigh before you train. I've booked for you to fight Charlie Miller at the Belle Vue, Manchester, on Monday.'

The boxing show at the Belle Vue, was promoted by Londoner, Harry Levine, and my opponent Charlie Miller was a Manchester fighter having his first pro fight. I'd usually be a couple of pounds over weight and Mac, looking at the scale said, 'Three pounds that's nothing. Friday today. You can lose a couple of pounds in the gym tonight, then dry out over the weekend and you'll come in dead on the weight Monday.' That saying was truer than he intended. Mac put an arm around my shoulders and said, 'Now listen to me, I know what I'm talking about, you'll be alright on Monday. You'll box the ears off this kid.'

I had a couple of rounds sparring, ten minutes skipping and some exercises before wiping myself (once again no showers) and getting dressed before Mac gave me a lift to the General Station where I caught a train home to Abercanaid.

The weekend before the fight, once again, I'd be unbearable to live with. Having little to eat and drying out, I'd be dehydrated and miserable. In bed at night I'd be having dreams of cream cakes and fizzy drinks. Finally the day of the show arrived and I travelled to Cardiff where Mac was waiting with a hired car.

The long drive to Manchester was tedious and gave me time to dwell on the fight and I was thinking, 'Had I lost too much weight in too short a time? Had I weakened myself in the process?' Finally, we arrived at the Belle Vue Manchester in time for the one o'clock weigh-in where I undressed and, holding my breath in apprehension, stepped onto the scale. To my relief I came in at the correct weight. I joined the queue of boxers to be checked by the doctor. I was introduced to my opponent and we headed for lunch at a nearby restaurant before visiting a cinema to rest for the afternoon. The evening of the show I was early on the bill and although a bit tense I felt good and ready for a fight. There was no mistaking my mood. I was out to win and win well. I stopped Miller in the fourth round, all for a purse of thirty pounds plus expenses.

Chapter 16

Sparring Partner

After I turned pro I was asked to help Howard Winstone and Ken Buchanan by being their sparring partner. Winstone, British and European Featherweight Champion, had failed in his attempts to take the World title off Mexican Vicente Saldivar, but was eventually destined to become World Featherweight Champion and one of Wales' greatest boxers. Ken Buchanan became World Lightweight Champion. I'd sparred with many good fighters over the years, all of whom I'd matched or even bettered, but Winstone and Buchanan proved to be in a class above them all.

Using my father's old, battered A35 van that neither of us was licenced to drive I got behind the wheel. My father sat in the passenger seat and we headed for Eddie Thomas' gym. On arriving at the building we made our way up the dark staircase where Eddie greeted us, 'Alright Bill, George?' We returned the greeting and went into the changing room to see Howard Winstone and another sparring partner getting ready for action. Again we exchanged greetings and I began to change as Eddie appeared and said to my father, 'Bill, will you give How' a rub down tonight?' My father was prepared for this and producing his bottle of magic oil said, 'Yep, I was going to anyway.'

Eddie stood in the corner of the dressing room waiting while we changed, donned our headgear, protectors and sparring gloves.

'You first George,' said Eddie. 'Two rounds, right!'

I followed Winstone into the boxing ring while the others stood watching.

'Off you go then,' said Eddie looking at his watch.

Some fighters prefer to 'Go easy' in sparring but with Winstone there were no holds barred and sparring with the champion was hard. The two rounds sparring finished and Eddie said, 'Out you get George. Ready Sam?' and the other sparring partner took my place in the ring. We changed places every two rounds to keep ourselves fresh and Winstone on his toes. Winstone sparred eight rounds before Eddie said it was enough. We skipped for twenty minutes, finished off with floor exercises and retired to the dressing room where my father gave Winstone and me a wipe with our towels and a rub down.

We all left the gym and while Eddie was locking the front door I asked him when I would get paid for the sparring. Eddie looked at me as if I'd asked him for a million pounds.

'When will you get paid?' he blurted out. 'You'll get paid the same time as everyone else, when Winst' has fought.'

I felt peeved that Eddie Thomas should talk down to me when all I did was ask him a simple question, which in all fairness was part of the business. After all, professional boxing is a business. It became clear to me that Eddie considered himself the gaffer and didn't like his fighters or any one else asking him for money. But I was having none of it.

'Oh ai,' I said, 'When's that then?'

Eddie started to rub his ear, appearing to think and said, 'Oh er straight after the fight, George. Oh, by the way, it's Mac I give your money to. He's your manager and I do the business with him.'

That was okay with me and I said as much.

Four nights a week for two weeks I sparred with Howard Winstone after which he fought and won his fight. It was my first sparring job and I was looking forward to collecting my hard earned wages so I phoned Mac and asked him to send me my money. But according to Mac, Eddie Thomas hadn't paid him. So I phoned Eddie but still couldn't get my sparring money.

I also spoke to Howard Winstone who told me he knew nothing of the financial matters concerning his boxing, only of what money he received after the fight. Mac Williams told me before each of my fights how much I was getting paid, and after the fight how much money was being deducted for expenses. I then discovered from some of Eddie's fighters that he paid them whenever he was ready to do so, which could be weeks or months after a contest. Finally, some of Eddie's boxers would be given a small amount of cash with no explanation of expenses. I wasn't happy with that news to say the least, and my father wasn't too happy about it either. Eventually, Eddie paid my father after he offered to intervene to speed things up. After that, all future sparring sessions were arranged between Eddie and me on the basis that the money was paid directly to me. Mac Williams didn't take any commission out of my sparring money.

After one such sparring session I waited until Winstone had fought then asked Eddie for my money. 'I'll see you in the gym Monday night,' said honest Eddie. Winstone's other sparring partner got wind of this and he arrived at the Penydarren gym the same time as I did. Eddie didn't turn up so I telephoned him at his home and he assured me that I would be paid in a day or two. I could not accept his proposal so I told him I wanted my money that night, and mentioned that the other sparring partner was waiting at the gym as well. To be fair, Eddie did pay me that night, but only after I stood up to him, which perhaps was unusual amongst his boxers.

Boxers belonging to the same setup as Winstone sparred with him for nothing, a practice not uncommon in the fight business where one stable mate would help another. But the majority of Eddie's boxers had to spar with Winstone most gym nights, with a lot having the boxing punched out of them before they even entered a contest. Fortunately for me, Winstone had been boxing as a pro for about six years when I started sparring with him. He was just starting to fade but I was able to learn from the great boxer. He still showed class and sparring with him was always hard. I'm sure that boxing buffs would agree that Ken Buchanan benefitted greatly from the fact that he was starting his career as Winstone was tailing off. Instead of Buchanan being punished as he started off his pro career, he learned. Winstone was sharp of wit and well known for practical jokes, but during training he worked hard, concentrated on what he had to do with all joking set aside. Ken Buchanan was in the same mould as Winstone when it came to training and they both become world champions because of it.

Most of my time, I trained at the Merthyr Labour Club along with Dai Harris, Les Picket, the Miles brothers and many other boxers under the guidance of my father who kept his eye on proceedings. I put my heart and soul into training and at home on the mountainside chopped wood to strengthen my arms, neck and shoulder muscles. Good fighters need supple, flexible muscles that can unleash in microseconds. I did little weight training because fighters who use excessive weights become muscle bound. Sparring is important in a build up to a fight and I travelled around the valleys to different gyms sparring with different fighters.

Being new to professional boxing I bought myself 14 ounce sparring gloves, that are normally used by heavyweights. Winstone, like most boxers used 10 ounce gloves to spar with, that were a lot smaller.

Now the thing is, sparring with the world champion was hard work anyway, but with me wearing gloves a lot bigger I was asking for trouble. Winstone was always annoyed about having to pay someone to spar with him so he'd really go to town on a paid sparring partner, making him work hard for the money. After one hard session Winstone cut up rough and I went home bruised and bleeding. A few days later at Mac Williams' gym I told him about the sparring only to get an earful from the Cardiff man. 'What the bleeding hell are you wearing big gloves for,' he yelled at me. 'You are bleeding well asking to be bumped about.' Mac walked to a cupboard in the gym, took out a pair of boxing gloves and threw them to me. 'Wear them a few times,' he said. I tried on the 10 ounce gloves, so hardened it was like putting wooden clubs on my hands. I thought, 'Oh boy,' just one sparring session and then I'd buy myself some new gloves.

The following week at the Penydarren gym Winstone and I climbed into the ring and started sparring. Bang! Every time I hit him it was as if I'd hit him with a hammer. At the end of two rounds Winstone was bruised and spitting blood, bouncing with temper and shouting, 'One more round.'

'Right,' said Eddie, 'Have one more.'

The next round was the same, more blood coming out of the champion's mouth and Winstone now seething with rage and saying, 'One more round.'

But Eddie had seen enough and ordered us out of the ring. I put the hardened boxing gloves in my bag, finished training and left the gym. The following night I again turned up for sparring, walked into the dressing room and started to change. I could see Eddie and Winstone talking together. 'Hang on, George,' said Eddie, 'Let's have a look at those gloves.'

I went into my bag and pulled out a pair of new sparring gloves. 'Oh, they look all right,' spouted Eddie.

Nothing more was said about the incident. We both respected each other and did our job. There was never any let up by either of us, but that's the way it was. Winstone was a true professional and became World Champion because of it.

Chapter 17

Boxing at the National Sporting Club

Sparring with Howard Winstone and Ken Buchanan meant that sometimes Mac Williams would arrange for me to box on the same show. On one such occasion on the 10th October, 1966, Winstone was fighting American, Don Johnson at the Free Trade Hall Manchester, and Mac booked me to fight on the same bill against Manchester's Gerry McBride. Mac, being unable to travel, asked Eddie to look after me. Eddie Thomas, Winstone and I travelled by car and arrived at the hotel in Manchester where I discovered nobody had booked me a room. The result was having to share a bed with Winstone. After my sleepless night listening to Winstone snoring, we were called for a light breakfast of tea and toast, then spent a couple of hours viewing part of Manchester before attending the one o'clock weigh-in, after which we had lunch and rested during the afternoon. The evening soon came around and Eddie took us to the show where we found the dressing room and got changed ready to box.

I was first on the bill. Eddie bandaged and taped my hands and we made our way into the hall where the Manchester fans were clapping and cheering McBride who was climbing into the boxing ring. I accepted that fighting a local man wasn't going to be easy, but although I was just beginning my pro career I'd won all my fights and was feeling confident. I climbed into the boxing ring and the MC made the introductions. Then the referee called McBride and me to the centre of the ring and gave us our instructions. We returned to our corners and the bell sounded to start the fight. Halfway through the first round I had a feeling that I was going to be the better fighter and although McBride boxed well I was getting the better of him in exchanges and beating him to the punch. The second round went my way but during the third I slipped and fell and the crowd started shouting for McBride. But the applauding stopped when I regained my composure and started out-boxing him again. When the home crowd goes quiet it's a sign that the local lad is losing and that is exactly what happened during the next couple of rounds. When the bell rang to end the sixth and last round I walked to the referee expecting him to hold up my arm as winner. But, to my surprise and everybody else's, the ref gave the decision to McBride, who was immediately booed by his own Manchester crowd. What a terrible decision and so badly received by McBride's own crowd that they booed him out of the ring. Later, while I was in the dressing room, the ref called to see me to make sure there were no hard feelings. He was a young ref from Manchester who felt obliged to give the home lad the decision. He obviously felt relieved of guilt by shaking my hand. I shrugged my shoulders and didn't bother to reply.

Since Mac Williams, was not at the show, I had to look after my own financial affairs and the fight. I phoned to tell him the result. 'Mac, I lost but I was bloody robbed.'

'Yes, I know,' said Mac, 'I just saw it on telly, I didn't know it was to be televised. You're entitled to more money.' Mac started shouting down the phone. 'George you've got to ask the promoter for more money yourself. If you leave it until after tonight they won't pay you.'

So, along with my brother-in-law, Malcolm Smith, who was with me, I went to look for the Demmy brothers who were the promoters and found them in an office at the front of the hall. Guarding the office door was a big man and I asked him if I could see Mr Demmy. The guard opened the door, mumbled a few words to somebody inside then turned to us and said, 'Go in.'

I will never forget the sight that met my eyes. Behind a large table, piled high with money, stood Gus Demmy and his brother, counting. (You must remember that in those days, a boxer's share of TV revenues was a new concept, and although it seemed unfair, a boxer in my position couldn't really expect very much more from the promoter. Things now of course, have swung dramatically the other way.)

Every so often, someone carrying a brown paper carrier bag came into the room and emptied a pile of money onto the table. After a while, one of the Demmy brothers came around the table and asked me what I wanted. I explained about the TV and asked him if I could have more money (please Mr Demmy). Ten pounds was put in my hand and I was shown out of the room, just as someone else was tipping another carrier bag of money onto the table.

I was still boxing six rounds when, on the 28th November, 1966 I was matched against Johnny Radcliffe, at the National Sporting Club. It was my first fight at the NSC and I wanted to impress the London crowd. The London razmataz was exciting and the Café Royale on Regent Street where the Sporting Club was located had a doorman wearing a top hat and tails while inside, the waiters wore Dickie bows. The boxing crowd was always buzzing with smart arses in suits, many talking about boxing as if they had invented the game.

On the Monday morning, the day of the show, my father and I travelled to Cardiff where Mac was waiting for us. The drive to London was long and tedious giving me plenty of time to dwell on the fight. Once again, I had had to lose about seven pounds to make the weight. I was now a Lightweight fighting around 9st 10lbs, but I weighed about 10 stones and it was a constant worry, would I make the weight, had I weakened myself? When, at last, we arrived in London, Mac drove into Soho and parked the car (hefty parking fees). We made our way to the Café Royale and headed for the lift. Mac, who hadn't stopped talking, asked the liftboy for the fourth floor where the boxing and weigh-in were to be held. The lift started rising, and when it stopped the boy said, 'Fourth floor,' as he pressed a button and opened the door. Mac thanked him and pressed a tip into his hand. I didn't mind but all the expenses were taken out of my fight money.

Inside the dressing rooms were other boxers stripping off ready to be weighed and be seen by the doctor. Walking around were the reps, Les Roberts the matchmaker, newspaper reporters, managers talking about fights and money and a lot of other people I didn't think had any business there at all. Mac, now champing an unlit cigar said, 'Right George, strip off.'

The BBBC rep, ticking his list said, 'On the scale then, son. What's your name again?'

I told him my name, stepped onto the weighing machine and held my breath, 'Nine stone ten pounds,' the inspector said as he marked his sheet of paper.

Mac breathed a sigh of relief and said, 'There, I told you not to worry didn't I. Right George, go and see the Doc and we'll be off.'

Mac, who didn't seem at all bothered, turned and chased across the room in search of someone else to talk to while I got dressed in peace. By this time I was so thirsty after drying out for a couple of days that all I could think about was getting something to drink. I picked up my gear, called my manager who was bending someone's ear, 'Come on Mac, I'm going,' and with my father headed for the stairs, not bothering with the lift that I'd have to wait for and probably give another tip. Mac came running after me shouting, ''Ang on, what's the bleeding hurry?'

Leaving the Café Royale, I stopped to buy a small bottle of

pop from a stand on the pavement. I couldn't remove the metal top from the bottle and in my frustration I hit it against the wall, breaking the top and tipping the contents down my throat. I walked to the Regent Palace Hotel where I booked a room to rest for the afternoon, then into Soho to find a restaurant for lunch. As we walked along the pavement Mac caught hold of my arm and said, 'Come on, let's go into Topo Gigio.' Inside the restaurant, my chattering manager acknowledged everyone and I thought he couldn't possibly know them all. A light lunch was ordered for me and my father and a large steak and bottle of red wine for Mac. After the meal Mac paid his compliments to the waiter. 'Lovely meal, as usual, Mario,' and pressed a large tip into his hand.

Outside Topo Gigio's Mac gave the orders. 'Right George, back to the hotel. Get your head down and I'll call for you about eight, Okay.' Mac then disappeared into the Soho crowd.

With my father I made my way to the hotel, stopping to look into shop windows and admire young girls as they flaunted the new fashions. At the hotel I collected the room key, and while my father headed for the TV lounge I took a lift to the required floor, found the room and lay on the bed trying not to think of the fight. But I was worried about having lost so much weight. What if I had weakened myself by losing so much in such a short time? No fighter is too concerned about getting hurt. He accepts the situation. What a fighter worries about is performing badly in front of a crowd and losing the fight. It seemed like no time at all before Mac was knocking on the door and as soon as he entered the room he said, 'Get your gear then let's go.'

Once I'd dressed, we called my father, walked to the Café Royale and once again headed for the lift to the fourth floor. The dressing rooms were a hive of activity as managers were taping their boxer's hands and people rushed around. We found a couple of empty chairs. I stripped off and Mac taped my hands before rubbing Vaseline all over my body. I hated having grease on my body; it was so difficult to remove after the fight without having showers to use. But, a grease covering was essential to help stop abrasions. There were three other fighters sharing the dressing room and we all sat like gladiators waiting to be called into the arena. Many of the patrons in the hall knew nothing about boxing and to them it was just a night of eats, booze and business.

The whip appeared and asked for one of the fighters who was on first bout. He started shadow boxing to warm up. Then, following his manager he left the room for the walk into the hall. We could hear the announcements and applause, then the bell to start the fight. After what seemed like no time at all, the same boy was being helped back into the dressing room concussed, and bleeding profusely from one of his eyebrows. The doctor arrived and looked at the cut before searching in his bag for medical equipment, then began stitching the wound.

Billy, the whip, appeared again, looked at Mac and said, 'Your boy's on next Mac, Okay.' Then looking at me said, 'On next son.' Mac tried to answer but with cotton buds sticking out of his mouth could only mutter, 'Yea yea.' Ten minutes later the whip appeared again, hurried across to where we were and said, 'Are you ready, son? You'll have to hurry. They're waiting.' Mac was sweating profusely as he grabbed hold of his bag of gear and said, 'Come on let's go.'

We walked through the crowd of club members who had just finished their meal and were now drinking wine, laughing and joking. I entered the ring from one side, and my opponent from the other. We stood in our own corners while the MC made the announcement. 'My Lords, Gentlemen, the first bout of the evening is a lightweight contest over six three minute rounds between from Merthyr Tydfil, in South Wales, George Evans.' There was clapping from club members. 'And from Bournemouth, Johnny Radcliffe.' There came another round of light applause. I wiped my boxing boots in a tray of resin and Mac held the water bottle for me to rinse my mouth. Mac was still sweating and with cotton buds behind his ear said, 'Keep on your toes, keep your jab going and move around the ring.'

The referee called us fighters to the ring centre where he reminded us of the rules, ending with, 'Right, go back to your corners and when you hear the bell, come out fighting.'

The bell sounded, I walked to the centre of the ring to face my opponent and the fight began. Two young fighters having their first contest at the NSC wanted to impress and we went to war. Radcliffe was shorter than me and frequently pushed his head beneath my chin. I didn't realize it then, but many people who attended the boxing at the NSC were there mainly to do business and were not really interested in the boxing. But that night all present were spellbound by our six round contest.

There was no let up by either Radcliffe or me, toe to toe fighting for six hard rounds, by the last of which I was exhausted and could hardly stand but pride kept me going. Finally, the sound of the bell ended the last round bringing with it relief to us both. The ref raised my arm as winner. I was on cloud nine. After waiting to hear the MC announce me the winner on points, I left the ring, leaving corner hands to collect the nobbing (money) thrown into the ring by appreciative club members who had followed the age old custom of rewarding boxers who had taken part in a pleasing contest. Radcliffe and I would share it out later. As a crowd pleaser, I would frequently earn money that way. As I passed between tables on my way back to the dressing room club members tapped me on the back and said, 'Well done son, well done.'

Back in the dressing room Mac and I shook hands before I started to wipe as much of the grease off my body as possible. Then Mac disappeared to look for the matchmaker who would pay the night's fight money. Before we left for home, Mac always sorted the money so that I was paid that same day. I had performed well and would be invited back to box at the NSC.

In the audience that night, as guest of honour, was film star, Jack Palance. He was so impressed by my performance that he climbed into the ring and made a speech, saying it was one of the best fights he had ever seen and asked if he could meet me. The Sporting club matchmaker came into the dressing room and asked if I'd be a willing to meet the film star. Me, meet Jack Palance? Of course, I'd meet him, and when the big man came into the dressing room I was completely overawed.

Chapter 18

Boxing at Afan Lido

The following week, on 7th December, 1966 Howard Winstone was defending his British Featherweight title against Lenny (the Lion) Williams at the Afan Lido, Aberafon, a coastal town eight miles from Swansea.

Once again I'd been sparring with Winstone and was hoping to be on the same bill but the night before the show, Mac phoned to say that he was unable to get me a match. I was going to watch the boxing at the Afan Lido, and not wanting to miss a day's training I went for an early morning run. Later that same day, Mac Williams phoned me at the Steel Works to say I was to box a return fight with Johnny Radcliffe that evening on the Winstone v Williams show. 'Mac, I can't fight,' I shouted down the phone. 'I've been running this morning.'

'George, you've got to fight. It's all arranged,' said Mac.

Oh, my God! How the hell could I put up a good performance after I'd been training on the same day?

I turned up at the Afan Lido that evening expecting another tough fight. The hall was packed with fans expecting a good fight between Howard Winstone and hard punching Lenny Williams. With my father following I entered the dressing room and started to get changed, feeling a little depressed about taking the fight at such short notice. I was first on the bill and that suited me; get it out of the way. But I wasn't going to get caught up in a war just to please the audience, I'd use my skills and box like I knew how.

Once I was changed, taped and gloved up, the whip appeared and asked if I was ready. I nodded to Mac and my father, and followed them into the arena where I entered the ring and faced my opponent. The MC announced the contest to rapturous applause from the crowd. The referee checked our gloves before calling us to the centre of the ring. We went back to our corners and the bell sounded to start the first round. I'm sure Radcliffe felt the same way as I did about fighting that night.

He moved forward to meet me head on but I didn't oblige him but instead delivered two left jabs to his face that jolted his head. I then moved to the side and hit him with a right hand. My opponent chased after me. That was what I wanted because I stopped him short with a left jab and right cross. Each time Radcliffe tried to mix it, I boxed, catching him with lefts and rights and as the round ended I sensed that I had the edge. I continued to box and deliver some heavy punches until during the third round the ref stopped the contest to save Radcliffe from taking further punishment. I was on top of the world. Not only had I won, but in front of a mainly Welsh crowd as well. All the worrying I had done was for nothing. In fact, I think I boxed better because of the situation. That same night, Howard Winstone also stopped Lenny Williams to retain his titles.

My next contest was the 30th Jan, 1967 at the Wyvern Sporting Club, Manchester against Vic Woodhall. I won the fight when the ref stopped the contest in the fourth round to save Woodhall from taking further punishmen.

For my next fight I returned to the NSC on 20th March. Like most fighters, I disliked boxing on Sporting Club shows which always started late. This sometimes meant that boxers did not leave the venue until the early hours. On a lot of Sporting Club shows I was a supporting bout, usually last on the bill. After the contest I'd change, and it was past midnight by the time I made my way to Paddington Station to sometimes find that the train for Cardiff had left, leaving me with no hope of arriving home in Merthyr at a reasonable time. Travelling by car was more convenient but a very tiring journey, especially going home. Travelling by train was much more relaxing, but I had to make sure to catch the last passenger train to South Wales. If I did miss the last passenger train to Cardiff a milk train with a sleeper carriage attached arrived at Paddington Station late at night for a quick stop. The drawbacks were that passengers were not allowed to board at Paddington, and because the train travelled around the countryside, it took five hours to reach Cardiff.

Many times Mac, my father and I travelled on the underground from Piccadilly to Paddington, we'd scramble off the underground and run up the escalator to the station platform, trying to catch the milk train before it left. As we dodged between luggage trolleys so the stationmaster wouldn't see us, Mac would shout. 'Gimme money, George'. He needed to bribe the guardsman on the sleeper. The fee was five pounds per person, for which we could have a bed and a call at Newport Station with a cup of tea and toast before the train reached Cardiff General Station.

Occasionally I'd travel to Paddington alone and after the show there would be one mad rush from the boxing venue to the station where I'd see the last train for Cardiff disappearing down the track. I'd walk back out of the station to a hotel in Paddington. I'd pass a fiver to the night porter who'd allow me to sleep on one of the lounge chairs and wake me at 7am with toast and a cup of tea ready to catch the first train home. My purse money for boxing as a six rounder then was around thirty-five pounds before expenses.

I then progressed to travelling to London the day before the fight. Boy oh boy! Those were the days, when I'd book into a hotel in Sussex Gardens, Paddington. Five pounds a night bed only, a single room, barely furnished, situated at the top of the building (no lift). There would be old army blankets on the creaking bed, wallpaper peeling off the walls and one single light bulb hanging from a dirty-whitewashed ceiling.

I arrived at the steel works and as soon as I sat behind my desk the phone rang. 'Hello George, it's Mac, I've fixed it for you to box eight rounds at the World Sporting Club on Monday.' Promoter Jack Solomons based the World Sporting Club at the Grosvenor House hotel on Park Lane. Mac and I arrived in London the following week. I attended the weigh-in, had lunch and retired for the afternoon to the Regent's Palace hotel. I was taking it easy, lying on the bed in the hotel room when there was knock on the door. I wondered who would be calling at that time and opened the door to see two black guys who introduced themselves as retired American fighter Sandy Saddler, and American fighter Ulysses Jiminez who was topping the bill at the World Sporting club that night. They said that Solomons had told them to visit me at the hotel and that I would look after them! I welcomed them both and Sandy Saddler, who said he had business to attend to asked me to take Jiminez to a restaurant for lunch. It turned out that the American didn't like English food and spoke very little English! What a time we had traipsing around Soho looking for a suitable restaurant for Jiminez to eat at. But I just couldn't find one to suit him. After an hour had passed we arrived back at the hotel with the American still not having eaten and me exhausted. After travelling from South Wales in the morning, attending the weigh-in and going to the hotel, the last thing I wanted was to spend an hour trudging the streets.

Finally, Mac and Sandy Saddler called to take Jiminez and me to the fights. Once again, I was boxing a supporting bout and by the time the last bout came around I was almost asleep. My opponent had the advantage of living in London while I had travelled from Wales. In the ring referee Harry Gibbs checked our gloves, we were introduced and the fight began. In the first round I boxed well, finding my distance while my opponent, a hard-hitting fighter tried to close in on me. In the second round he waded in to fight and instead of boxing I traded punches. We stood in the centre of the ring at a war when all of a sudden there was a clash of heads. I felt a sharp pain over my eye and blood started running down my face. I knew I'd been cut, and badly. I tried to box but on seeing the blood he stormed in to make a fight of it. When the bell rang to end the round I sat on the stool and Mac shouted to the corner man assisting. 'No water, I need the minute to stop the bleeding.' Normally, during the minute interval, the fighter is given water to swill and freshen his mouth. The bell rang to start round three and I boxed and moved around trying to avoid a confrontation that would start the cut bleeding again. Halfway through the round my opponent waded in and I was fighting him off when there was another clash of heads and I was cut over the other eye. When the round ended I sat in the corner and the ref came over to me and said, 'Look son, stick to your boxing. If you mix it the eyes will bleed and I'll stop the fight.'

I nodded and Mac said, 'Yea, yea, thanks,' and the bell sounded to start the next round. During the fourth round I boxed and was beating the Londoner to the punch but towards the end of the round he waded in, I turned him but his glove caught my eyebrow and the cut started bleeding again. Without a second look the ref stopped the fight.

It was the early hours of the morning when Mac and I finally started for home. By the time I had dropped Mac off at his house in Cardiff, I had another hour's driving to get to Abercanaid where I'd grab an hour's sleep before going to the steel works.

Chapter 19

Welsh Boxing Council

During the 1960s-70s the bright lights of London were exciting and everything about the vast city fascinating for a Welsh Valley boy. The flower people only wanted to love each other and Sandy Shaw kicked her shoes off to sing. There was the smell of a hot dog stand on Piccadilly, where I had an argument with the stall holder because he wanted to charge me 7/6 for a 2/6 bottle of coke.

When boxing at plush venues like the Grosvenor House Hotel, the Hilton Hotel and Café Royale, I'd stand outside watching the patrons arrive by Rolls Royce and Mercedes, wondering how there could be so many wealthy people in London. I stayed in bigger hotels that were a far cry from the tiny little rooms in Sussex Gardens, where I had stayed when I first turned pro. I was fighting eight round contests, earning, on average, about eighty pounds for each fight and after paying expenses and manager's fee taking home about forty pounds.

Many different characters attended boxing shows including top businessmen involved in legitimate practices, and racketeers like the Kray twins. There were the bums and the spivs, all wanting to be around the world of boxing, and the high class prostitutes who'd walk through big hotels like royalty.

Les Roberts, matchmaker of the National Sporting Club,

keen to keep his prized job and all the glamour and money that went with it, had to keep the Sporting Club patrons happy and regularly attending club shows, and so, he used the likes of Ken Buchanan to top the NSC bill as a draw. The NSC, being a private concern attracted little publicity and as a result top boxers who fought there regularly were still virtually unknown, and I suspect, earned little money until they reached World status. Some well-known hotels that held boxing shows were as extravagant and plush as you would expect in such establishments. But the dressing rooms reserved for boxers at these places left a lot to be desired, with many providing only a small room with no washing facilities and frequently no furniture.

Many Welsh boxers were overmatched to keep the London fighters winning and NSC members happy. It became apparent to me that many managers and promoters regarded boxers as a disposable commodity. I suffered because of this when, after I'd fought a couple of six round contests I was matched against former British Lightweight Champion, Jimmy Revie, at the NSC. At that time, Revie had recorded ten fights, ten wins, ten knockouts. I was stopped on a cut eye in the second round. Back in the dressing room, a doctor put stitches in my eyebrow, gave me a quick examination and left. After that fight the cuts over my left eye worsened and more often than not, win or lose I would cut. I will always remember the look of terror on Hilary's face when she saw the facial cuts and bruises when I arrived home.

In July 1968 Mac Williams arranged for me to box on a show at the Manor Place Baths, London, where, during the Victorian era women of means would bathe and pay young boys to wash and massage them. Mac was unable to travel and so once again I journeyed alone and booked a hotel room where I'd rest for a couple of hours before boxing. The weigh-in went okay and I returned to the West End for a meal. Because I was alone, I couldn't resist seeing the sights and spent the next hour or so walking around instead of resting.

Evening arrived and I made my way to the venue and found the dressing room. I needed someone to tape my hands, glove me up and assist me in the corner during my fight and so I looked around and saw Phil Edwards, former top middleweight boxer from Cardiff who was managing one of the boxers fighting on the same bill. I asked Phil if he'd help me and the likeable Phil readily agreed. Phil's boxer, also from Cardiff, was first on the bill. I was boxing second bout so Phil taped and gloved us both, with the idea that after his boxer had fought and returned to the dressing room with his trainer, Phil would remain in the corner ready to help me. His boxer climbed into the ring and the usual formalities and introductions took place before the bell rang to start the first round. The Cardiff boxer moved around, jabbing at his opponent who frequently retaliated, and the round ended fairly evenly. The next round started well enough until a thunderous right hand caught Phil's boxer flush on the jaw and he fell like a sack of spuds, out like a light. The doctor was called to revive the Cardiff boxer and he was helped from the ring. Phil, all in a fluster, came running to me and said, 'Sorry George, I've got to look after my boxer, you'll have to find someone else to corner you.'

I quickly looked around the hall for a corner man. The MC was calling my name, asking me to enter the ring while I was in a panic rushing around asking different people to corner me. Fortunately, an unknown trainer stepped forward and offered to help.

I won the fight on points over eight rounds, but I had to drive home to Merthyr with one eye closed, stopping at Mac's house in Cardiff in the early hours to pay him the fee of 25% that he was entitled to.

We'd entered the year of 1968 and by this time I'd sussed out the boxing lark and the way it was being run. The two main players in Welsh boxing management, Eddie Thomas and Benny Jacobs, although having to kneel before the top London promoters for the big televised shows, had boxing sown up in Wales. They were constantly at each other's throats, knowing that whoever managed the better fighters more or less controlled Welsh boxing. A fighter originally signed a boxer-manager contract for seven years which was almost all of a boxer's fighting life. If, after signing a contract, a boxer felt that he was being badly treated by his manager he could complain to the Welsh Area Council of the British Boxing Board of Control. But complaining to the Board would be pointless because the Welsh Area Council was made up of licenced members, including managers and promoters who were often the same people.

It was well known that Eddie Thomas and Benny Jacobs disliked each other and that Council meetings sometimes ended with them quarrelling. It was important for boxing people to attend these meetings and even more important for managers to have cronies on the Council to vote in favour of any recommendations put forward by them.

Mac Williams, keen to be of equal status to Eddie Thomas and Benny Jacobs, needed allies on the Council to vote for his recommendations and he encouraged me to become boxers' representative. Once enrolled onto the Council I was expected to attend the monthly meetings that were always held on a Thursday night in the Royal Hotel, St Mary Street, Cardiff, to sit among other members and vote when Mac gave me the nod. But I was rather independent and would only use my vote if I thought it right.

Mixing with the boxing crowd gave me a buzz and keen to be involved I'd arrive early at the Royal Hotel, conveniently situated near the main bus and railway stations. I'd enter the large foyer and see the friendly face of a 'Western Mail and Echo' sports writer, either Tom Lyons, Karl Woodward or Gareth Jones whom I'd have a chat with. Then I'd shake hands with Benny Jacobs who was also early and sitting with a number of his boxing cronies waiting to see who else attended the meeting.

After a spell of watching the main entrance, Benny, followed by his henchmen would leave the foyer and walk to the bar at the back of the hotel to see who had arrived that way. When he saw Eddie Thomas, Benny would grunt in satisfaction at having seen the enemy and walk back into the foyer. Someone would say, 'They're going upstairs' (meaning the committee), and those attending would follow them to the meeting room.

Being on the Council gave me chance to witness the goings on that can only be described as hilarious. The Marx brothers would have applauded the efforts of Eddie Thomas and Benny Jacobs as they tried to out-do each other. It went from one to the other, both trying to gain the upper hand. Eddie would put forward a proposal, relying on his chosen members to back him with their votes. Benny would object and expect his cronies to vote for him, and vice versa. The Council would reassert itself with the chairman saying, 'All those in favour,' and there'd be a show of hands resulting in another slanging match between Eddie and Benny. But whatever the two Welsh boxing managers thought of each other, they both knew they relied on the Welsh Council.

At one particular meeting, I entered the room to see the committee sitting and waiting. The room soon filled with licenced members. Benny Jacobs, holding onto a piece of paper he'd been making notes on, sat with his little gang in the front row on one side of the room, while Eddie and his crowd sat on the opposite side.

I sat at the back. There was a call to order from the chairman and the meeting began. It was always a friendly start. Several topics were discussed and Benny continually interrupted in order to make his opinions known. The banter started to hot up with the usual friendly rivalry that existed between the Valley people and Cardiffians. Eddie Thomas, not being quick witted enough to compete verbally with Benny Jacobs, became frustrated. In the meantime, the chairman, unsuccessfully, kept asking for order. He finally flared up and told Benny Jacobs to, 'Shut up you silly old bastard.' As quick as a flash Benny leaped from his chair, jumped across the table and grabbed hold of the chairman. Pandemonium reigned as Benny Jacobs was quickly restrained, and Eddie Thomas kept saying, 'I should throw him out of the window.'

Another farcical evening.

Chapter 20

Retired from Fighting

I had been boxing as a pro for two years, mainly training at my father's gym in the Merthyr Labour Club, but frequently travelling to other gyms. I was still sparring with Ken Buchanan and Howard Winstone, learning and getting paid at the same time. But I noticed things were changing at Eddie's Penydarren gym with the once friendly atmosphere beginning to sour, and what used to be one of the busiest gyms in the country was now quiet, with only Winstone or Buchanan training. There was a strained relationship between Eddie and Ken Buchanan. Howard Winstone, although obviously unhappy, put on a brave face and concentrated on training. His one wish was to win the title that had eluded him for so long and become World Featherweight Champion. After three unsuccessful attempts to take the title from Mexican Vicente Saldivar, the champion retired, leaving the title vacant.

The ruling World Boxing Organisation declared that Howard Winstone and Japan's Mitsunori Seki should challenge for the World Featherweight Title. Because the syndicate whose members were Harry Lavine, Micky Duff, Mike Barrett, Terry Lawless and Alex Steen were the only promoters able to clinch the title fight for Winstone in Britain, it was agreed with Eddie, that if Winstone should win, the first defence of his title would be for the London promoters.

Once again I'd been helping Winstone with his sparring and Mac Williams arranged for me to box on the same show at the Albert Hall on the 24th January, 1968. I was thrilled to be boxing at that top venue, matched against Tom McNeill over eight rounds. For this fight I was paid eighty-five pounds and, after paying my manager's fee and expenses, I took home forty-five pounds.

We'd spent the day in London, and in the early evening made our way to the Albert Hall where the news came that I was last on the bill. I was disappointed, because I wanted to fight before Winstone and then watch him box for the World Title. Twenty minutes before the show started, matchmaker Mickey Duff walked into the dressing room and I asked him if I could box before Winstone.

'Okay, George,' he said, 'I'll change the Bill and put you on first.'

I was overjoyed. I got changed and had my hands taped and gloved all inside ten minutes. I climbed into the boxing ring and fought eight rounds that I won on points in front of a large crowd which included many people from Merthyr. Later that evening, after five long years as a top boxer, Winstone became World Champion by stopping Mitsunori Seki. What a great occasion for Howard Winstone, Merthyr Tydfil, Wales and Britain.

Howard Winstone, World Featherweight Champion took a short break from boxing before starting to train for his first title defence. Eddie Thomas, no doubt manipulated by others, reneged on his deal with the syndicate and joined Jack Solomons and NSC matchmaker Les Roberts to promote Winstone's first defence of his title. Gullible Eddie was unable to see the serious consequences of his actions. In retaliation, Harry Levine Promotions, the biggest in Britain, would have nothing more to do with Eddie Thomas. Eddie's boxers were now unable to get fights on the big shows. This was particularly bad for Ken Buchanan who was a champion in the making, but could now only to box on small club shows for small money.

In the meantime, Welshman Howard Winstone was World Featherweight Champion and, despite all the behind the scenes wrangling, he, after a layoff started training for the defence of his title. The scene was set and Winstone was to defend his newly won crown against Spain's Jose Legra at Porthcawl, on the 24th July, 1968.

As usual, I was asked to help with sparring and arrangements were made for me to accompany Eddie and Winstone to a training camp in Carmarthen. For some reason, Eddie Thomas had begun to doubt his own training abilities and engaged trainer Archie Rule. He, in my opinion, wasn't as good as Eddie. But, the phenomenal Winstone, top boxer for an incredible seven years could not keep Old Father Time at bay and was having weight problems. Although he still had plenty of heart at twenty-seven years old and ten years pro boxing that included three epic battles against the great Saldivar, Winstone was beginning to show signs of slowing.

The fact that Winstone was no longer the man he was came as a shock to me during our sparring session at Carmarthen. I noticed before the fight that Winstone ate little, drank less fluid and kept sucking lemons in an attempt to reduce weight. I had spent years losing weight in this way and knew how daunting it could be in a build up to a fight. The harmful effects of dehydration could be serious both mentally and physically. At the hall where the sparring session was being held Winstone and I changed, climbed into the ring and started our customary ten minutes skipping to warm up. Then we gloved ready to spar. Eddie was in one corner attending Winstone and Archie Rule in the other corner looking after me. The bell sounded and we started sparring. I was surprised how easy it was to beat Winstone to the punch. When the round ended I went back to the corner and Archie Rule kept saying, 'You're beating him to the punch. If you don't stop beating him, they'll sack you.' Archie Rule, being slightly deaf was talking loudly enough for everyone, including Eddie, to hear. The bell sounded for the next round, but how can you not punch a great fighter who keeps coming for you. Eddie had seen enough. 'That's it George,' he said. Another sparring partner took over my role and I was taken back to Merthyr.

I was at Porthcawl to watch Howard Winstone sadly lose his World Title to Jose Legra of Spain. Winstone sustained an eye injury that forced the referee to stop the fight.

Having lost his World Title Howard Winstone, retired from boxing. It was as if the heart had been taken out of Eddie's Penydarren gym and it become deserted. I was still engaged as sparring partner for Ken Buchanan who, although trained by his father in Scotland, finished off his training in Merthyr. Buchanan, like Winstone, was a world class fighter and sparring with him never easy. It was obvious that Eddie and Buchanan weren't getting on and Eddie was rarely in the gym when Buchanan trained there. The Penydarren gym that had once buzzed with activity now only accommodated Ken Buchanan and me sparring and with Roy Seers timing us. Buchanan became World Lightweight Champion and it was only a matter of time before he would split with Eddie Thomas.

On top of it all, long time partner in crime Les Roberts fell out with Eddie in a big way. Les claimed that he had been instrumental in persuading Ken Buchanan to sign with Eddie, and it had supposedly been agreed that if Buchanan fought for a world title, then Eddie would give Les 10% of the purse money. But, according to Les Roberts, Eddie Thomas once again reneged on a deal and wouldn't pay. A bitter Les Roberts, told all and sundry about what he claimed was Eddie's treachery. As a result, Eddie's fighters couldn't get work at the National Sporting Club either.

I continued to box and toured the country to fights. But it was getting to be a drag as I approached my thirtieth birthday and the training was becoming a real bind. It got to the stage where I'd pay a doctor to give me two pain killing injections in each hand before I fought. My hands had taken so much of a battering during a lifetime's fighting that each punch I delivered caused pain to shoot up my hands and arms. Many times, during the long journey home from a fight that I had perhaps lost on cut eyes, I promised myself to pack in fighting. But, the following day, I'd remember that the car tax and insurance had to be paid or the children needed new clothes and I'd phone Mac to get me another fight. I began to realize that like many fighters I was being trapped in the game and there was always the danger of fighting for too long and getting seriously injured.

I was still employed at the steel works while boxing. Hilary worked at Hoover's and we could afford to move to a bigger house. 14 Donald Street, lower down the village of Abercanaid became the new family home. It was a nice quiet area next to the park with a view across to the river that flowed between foliaged banks teeming with wildlife; across to the mountain and down the valley to Troedyrhiw.

Family life was necessary and important too. Deborah and Julie were growing up and needed the comfort and security of normal family life and so, Hilary and I endeavored to spend as much time as we could with them. At Abercanaid we made a point of being involved in village life. We joined the Carnival Committee and along with Deborah and Julie, Hilary and I would dress up and take part in the parades. Although Hilary and I worked, it was important to spend 'family' time with our daughters, taking them on shopping trips, to the seaside, and being with them as much as possible.

Deborah and Julie enjoyed village life and attended Abercanaid's Junior School, until they were old enough to move on to Afon Taf Comprehensive where they both succeeded and went on to University.

Hilary and I must have been somewhat ambitious because

our next move was to buy one of the village grocery stores. In the centre of the village was a busy corner shop where we bought our groceries. Betty, who owned the store, confided to Hilary that she was about to retire, and offered her the first chance to buy and explaining that it was a good little business. I approached the bank for a loan. The under-manager agreed to lend me the money, then spent the next twenty minutes telling me that his father had a shop and that in his opinion, it would be better for me to invest in some other type of business! What a plonker! On his stupid advice we decided not to buy the shop. Betty sold it to another Abercanaid woman who after six months approached us with an offer to sell us the then rundown business in April 1975. Hilary chose to take the business on. A hard worker with a good personality and cheerful outlook, she worked hard and the village store became successful.

I was coming to the end of my career as a professional boxer. With seven years professional boxing behind me, my eyebrows were cutting badly, my hands had become brittle from constant hitting and, all in all, I decided it was time to hang up my gloves. Professional boxing had been good to me. I had made a bit of money which gave us all a better lifestyle. I had travelled a lot, met interesting people, visited big cities in Britain and abroad, stayed at fine hotels and dined in famous restaurants. I recalled my first visit to London remembering how black and dirty all the buildings were, but now, owing to new policies, the city was being cleaned up. Soho used to be a dirty seedy place with litter strewn around the streets, mostly coming from the street markets that lined the narrow roads. There were homeless people lying over the Hotel grills benefitting from the hot air coming up from the basement. Street girls would be touting their trade from shop doorways while their pimps hung around keeping an eye on their investments.

Looking back over my boxing career I reflect on many things. 'If only' comes to mind but nobody can put the clock back. Sure, I would change a lot but wouldn't we all? My consolation is that the ups outweigh the downs.

Chapter 21

Boxing Manager

With champions Howard Winstone and Eddie Avoth retired from boxing and Ken Buchanan leaving the scene, Eddie Thomas was no longer managing a champion and he eventually closed his Penydarren gym.

Howard Winstone now had time to dwell on his past and realised (at last) that the people in boxing who should have looked after him had in fact tucked him up. The Merthyr marvel turned to drink for solace and so began his descent into an early grave. Feeling the need to share his torment, Winstone divulged to me his regrets at not having received the amount of money that was promised for his fights. Winstone's disappointment cultminated after his final contest, the defence of his world title. He had in Eddie's presence been promised the sum of fifteen thousand pounds by Jack Solomons. He was unhappy about that sum and even more so when he was given just eleven thousand pounds by his manager. I was bound to ask why, knowing the show was a financial success with the three partners, Solomons, Les Roberts and Eddie Thomas gloating about the money they were making, he hadn't told Solomons that he was unhappy with what he got. And why, when Eddie gave him eleven thousand, four thousand pounds short of what was promised, he hadn't asked Eddie to explain.

Winstone dropped his head and replied that he had never been able to confront Eddie or the man in charge, Jack Solomons. He was dominated by them and try as he might couldn't bring himself to face them with the facts.

For a long time it had been dawning on me that managing boxers would be far easier than fighting myself. After being active in the world of professional boxing, and getting acquainted with top boxing people, I retired from fighting, intending to apply for a manager's licence.

For decades, top boxing men from London had been drawn to Merthyr Tydfil by the smell of money.

Now that Eddie Thomas no longer managed any Merthyr boxers, I became the prime target to be governed by London promoters who needed someone else to manage Merthyr fighters that they could also control. I didn't realise it at the time, but Les Roberts was already making plans to use me through my former manager Mac Williams, who kept asking me to become his partner in managing boxers from Merthyr. But I had chosen to manage boxers by myself and, not realising the set-up between Mac Williams and Les Roberts, I confided my plans to the London matchmaker who told Mac, thus putting a strain on our relationship.

The fact is, that, as a boxer, I'd never had to do business directly with the boxing crowd, I took people on face value and trusted them, many times to my cost. I entered a world of conmen having to learn the hard way. Mac Williams and I had been friends for many years and he offered me a lot of advice in my early days of managing. I learned that when it comes to money and business one has few friends, only acquaintances.

When my mind was made up, looking for premises to house my own boxing gym became a priority. Opposite my in-laws home at Poplar Street, Troedyrhiw, stood the empty building that used to be an infants school where my wife Hilary had once been a pupil. It was worth sussing out and I took a look-see. The old, stone, Victorian style single story building consisted of an entrance room that led into a large assembly hall with high, cream painted walls, a white emulsioned ceiling and a wooden floor. Built into one of the walls was a large, Victorian, cast iron fire grate surrounded by an old iron fireguard. There was an attached building of communal toilets, a small room I assumed had been the head teacher's and a number of classrooms. The old building, empty for many years had started to decay. It smelled of damp and had huge cobwebs hanging from the rafters. Oh yes, it certainly brought back memories of past gyms I'd been to. In fact it was ideal and in my mind's eye I could see it full of boxers training.

In 1974 I moved into the former infants school and began to convert it into a boxing club. I put a full size platform-boxing ring in the large hall along with punch bags, punch balls and other training equipment. I hung boxing posters on the walls and the gym was ready for use. Joe Beckett who lived next door to my in-laws, entered the gym one night and became a good friend and assistant trainer stayed with me for the next twenty years. Old Joe, one of the mainstays in the gym, was a portly man with white hair and a friendly smile on his face. Soft of heart, he helped many and at times I'd enter the gym to see some bum sweeping the floor. Joe would explain that the sweeper needed money.

After eighteen months of running a successful amateur boxing club the time was right for me to apply for a manager's licence and look after professional boxers.

And so I reintroduced professional boxing to the village of Troedyrhiw and the Merthyr Valley. I would recall stories told by my father of regular boxing at Troedyrhiw Welfare Ground where among others, the Terrett brothers, Jack, Tom, Bob, Dick and Jim who once lived in Troedyrhiw, were well known for their boxing and fighting. The best boxer was probably Dick Terrett who, unfortunately, was forced to finish through ill health. Although never making it big, the Terrett brothers provided local entertainment.

Having decided to become a manager I needed a good fighter and he came in the shape of Merthyr's Welsh Amateur Lightweight Champion, John Wall. According to the norm, professional champions come from amateur champions and I was hoping it applied to my new signing. Although he was unlikely to emulate former world champion, Howard Winstone, I knew that Wall could become the local boxing talent. It was time for me to introduce myself as Merthyr's new boxing manager.

In a blaze of local publicity I was granted a manager's licence, John Wall a boxer's licence and the show was ready to roll. It was a new venture for us both and we wanted to prove ourselves worthy. The timing was right, Merthyr and Welsh boxing fans were without a good professional boxer to support and follow and John Wall was ready to step into the breach. My ambition to become a good boxing manager encouraged me to believe that John Wall would become a British Champion and my enthusiasm spilled out to boxing writers who reported my dreams in print.

Because John Wall became the media's focus of attention, the smell of money once again attracted top boxing men from London and the memory of all the money they had made out of Howard Winstone spurred them on.

Eddie Thomas, having read what I'd said to the newspapers believed in my dreams and informed Les Roberts and Jack Solomons. They, in turn, believed what Eddie told them because pound signs flashed in front of their eyes.

Their target this time was boxing manager, George Evans and his recently signed boxer, John Wall. I was offered the chance to become a pawn for the London boxing men but I wasn't so easily influenced. I became a stumbling block to some London matchmakers and promoters for refusing to accept inducements that would put me in their pockets. I already knew most of the top matchmakers and promoters, the majority of whom were respectable, but I was soon to meet the low life of the boxing world.

Promoters are keen to keep their boxers winning which is understandable, but some of the top promoters will go to amazing lengths to achieve this aim. A boxing manager might be tempted not do his job properly by allowing a matchmaker to arrange fights on his behalf, thus saving him considerable time and expense but allowing boxers to be exploited. Promoters and matchmakers, like Les Roberts of the National Sporting Club, Jack Solomons, Micky Duff and, in fact all of the top players would lean on managers to get their cooperation. But it was business and to be expected. To give and take is part of managing. But I believe that a lot of managers, for financial reward, do all the giving and always at the expense of the fighter. We all make mistakes, but making a mistake is not the same as being greedy. Boxers were being overmatched and beaten in order to accommodate promoters. Some promoters employed agents or matchmakers who were paid by results only. In order to acquire a match to suit the promoter's fighter they would lie, cheat and in the end offer so much money that it was very difficult to resist. The agent was matching the promoter's boxers and out to get them a win. Unfortunately, many boxing managers were only interested in the money and found it easier to answer the phone and accept the opponent offered for one of their fighters. The only question asked by the manager would be, 'How much are you offering?' The result was that few young boxers guided by those managers got very far. Sometimes a manager accepted a contest for one of his boxers fully understanding that he'd been overmatched and would lose the fight. The reason might be that the matchmaker had promised the manager an easy fight for another of his boxers on a different show. Being unable to tell the boy that he was expected to lose, the manager would try and arrange it so that the boxer was not fully prepared.

He might take his boxer for a meal too close to the fight and encourage him to eat too much, or just psych him out of a winning mood by telling him he wasn't fit. I am happy to say that I was never tempted to follow any of these practices but if I had, I could have made a lot more money out of boxing. Instead, I always tried to do my best for the fighters I managed and rarely took my manager's fee from a six round boxer. I also paid all travelling expenses for sparring. I didn't ever take my expenses in full from any boxer after he'd fought. I always paid my trainer and my companion and assistant trainer, Joe, out of my own pocket.

To be fair, many people involved in boxing are also respectable.

Eager and full of zest I started looking for an opponent for Wall's first pro fight, and after a number of weeks came up with unbeaten Londoner, Mark Bliss. It was to take place at Shoreditch Town Hall on the 28th January, 1975, the last show at this venue before its demolition. Although Bliss hadn't lost a pro fight, his style would suit John Wall who, I was convinced, would be too big and strong for the Londoner. After discussions with several boxing people I discovered that the Londoners knew little about Wall, and thought it would be another win for their man. Being too cocky put them at a disadvantage.

Wall was a good trainer and had plenty of time to get fit, but, after I had agreed the match, some doubt crept into my mind as to whether the handling of the fight would be fair. Had I made a mistake in taking a fight for Wall against an unbeaten London fighter whose handlers would do almost anything to keep their man winning? I had seen referees give bad decisions and I'd lost fights myself when given a bad decision.

Oh yes, this was what managing was all about, having to continually consider whether I'd made the right match for my fighter? Would he be properly prepared? Would he be fit? Would he make the weight? About myself I had no worries; about my fighter I had plenty.

The business had to be sorted and it was all go. A coach was hired to take Wall's fans to the show in London and the tickets ordered. The main thing however was to get Wall in peak condition for the contest. But, John Wall had one problem that was to remain with him for the whole of his boxing career; he always had difficulty making the weight.

I hired boxers to spar with him at my gym and as the date of the contest loomed nearer he was in top condition and ready to go. Then I again began to think about how so called friends in boxing had encouraged me to take the fight thinking that Wall would get knocked off, thus giving me a bad reputation and encouraging Merthyr fighters to sign with them. If I had to learn anything about the business it was not to trust too many boxing people.

Chapter 22

Shoreditch

Finally, the morning of the show arrived and I was as excited about Wall having his first pro fight as I had been about mine. Hilary had organised the coach to take the fans to the show but her first job that morning was to drive me to the garage where I'd hired a car. I drove the hired car to Dowlais to pick up John Wall, then on to Troedyrhiw to collect Joe and we were on our way to London. Wall was a bit nervous so I kept up the chatter to keep his mind off the fight, and a stop at a service station on the M4 seemed like a good idea. At the cafeteria we queued behind two fellows as they filled their plates with rashers of bacon, eggs and sausages. By the time they'd reached the checkout most of the food had been eaten and all they paid for were two sausages each! John Wall couldn't eat before the weigh-in so I paid three pounds for two coffees that tasted like cats' pee, and would only have cost me a pound in Merthyr. After a short break we continued on our way and arrived early, well in advance of the one o'clock weigh-in. I had travelled to London many times before but today seemed special.

On arriving at Shoreditch Town Hall, we mingled with other boxing people who were involved with the evening's show and I started to sort out the day's business. The room with the weighing scale was packed with newspaper reporters, boxers, managers, trainers, Boxing Board officials and others. Lined along the walls were chairs for the boxers' gear. A Boxing Board official stood by the scale holding a sheet of paper with the boxers' names, waiting for each fighter to step onto the scales.

Meanwhile a doctor arrived late and flustered about sorting his gear. The Official cleared his throat and looking around the packed room asked, 'Are Wall and Bliss ready?'

Mark Bliss appeared and stepped onto the scales. He was smaller than John Wall but looked lean and fit. He came in dead on the weight. The Official ticked his sheet of paper and shouted, 'John Wall.' I wasn't worried about Wall's weight, having already checked it the previous night. But when he stepped onto the scale, to my horror, he was one pound overweight. How the hell was he overweight? It could only be because he had eaten since I'd weighed him.

Fortunately for us, Mark Bliss's manager had never heard of Wall, and because he didn't consider him to be a good boxer he didn't take the fight too seriously. Instead of making Wall take the extra pound off he made a joke of it saying, 'Gotta pay a forfeit, a pound for a pound,' and laughed. But I had a feeling the joke would rebound on them.

But boy, was I relieved! I really could have done without that kind of scare. Wall was examined by the doctor and declared fit to fight. He got dressed and we left the old Town Hall. It was badly in need of decorating, but since it was due to be demolished, that was unlikely.

We climbed into the hired car and drove through lunchtime traffic to the West End and Soho, parked and booked a hotel for Wall to rest in the afternoon, then started looking for a tidy restaurant.

The routine was familiar to me and we soon settled into an eating-house where I made sure Wall didn't eat too much. Lunch eaten, we left the restaurant and headed for the hotel where Wall collected the room key. I'd return later and call him at about five o'clock, take him for a light tea and some toast then on to Shoreditch.

Joe and I had the afternoon to kill and, dodging the descending pidgin crap, we walked to Victoria Embankment, boarded the Caledonia Restaurant and sipped coffee as we discussed the day's events. As the afternoon wore on we left the embankment and walked to Piccadilly, heaving with tourists, some of whom were taking photos of Eros, the God of Love, as he stood on the fountain pointing his arrow.

We reached Shaftesbury Avenue, not going anywhere in particular, just talking as we strolled along when suddenly, a bloke carrying two suitcases stopped nearby. He up-ended one of the cases, placed the other flat on top and started shuffling three playing cards on it. Within minutes, a crowd had gathered to watch. 'Find the ace,' the bloke shouted as he moved the three cards about.

'I'll have a go,' said a man in the crowd as he put five tenners onto the case, turned one of the end cards over to reveal the ace.

'I won,' shouted the punter and was handed his winnings.

The dealer started moving the cards about again, clearly showing the ace as he placed it face down on the case. Someone else said, 'Forty pounds says it's the centre card.'

Once again the dealer turned the centre card over to reveal the ace and the man in the crowd was paid his winnings. The cards were moved around on top of the case once more and again, it could be seen clearly that the ace was put in the centre.

'Place your bets,' said the dealer and a man behind Joe tried to persuade him to bet fifty pounds saying, 'It's the centre card, mate, put fifty quid on. You're bound to win.'

But Joe refused to bet. A couple of blokes in the crowd did bet fifty pounds each and when the centre card was turned over it wasn't the ace at all and they lost their money. The dealer quickly pocketed the bets, picked up his cases and joined by his two henchmen from the crowd moved on down Shaftesbury Avenue looking for more suckers.

Moving on to Carnaby Street, we stopped for another cup of coffee before heading for the hotel where John Wall was resting. Joe waited in the hotel foyer while I went to Wall's room and found him ready and waiting. We went to a nearby restaurant where we had a snack and chat about the forthcoming fight, then onto Shoreditch Town Hall.

We arrived at the venue. There was another hour at least before the show was due to start but the hall was already beginning to fill with spectators. I found the dressing room and settled into a spot. More dressing rooms were being used by other fighters on the bill. Joe started to cut tape and stick it on the wall, ready for me to bandage John's hands before we put the gloves on him. I went looking for the matchmaker who told me that John Wall was on first. I was happy with that news because my boxer didn't have to hang about waiting and becoming nervous. But, was I a bag of nerves? I had thought waiting in the dressing room to fight when I was boxing was bad enough.

Wall had got changed and was waiting for me to bandage his mitts. I pulled an empty chair for him to put his hands over and wrapped bandage around his fists, then laid the cut lengths of tape over the back of his hands. While Joe put Vaseline over Wall's body I wandered out into the corridor, ignored two boxing managers arguing and went along to the main hall that was now full of people. A smile and nod from the muscular looking doorman who barred the entrance to those without a ticket, told me he realised who I was. I didn't enter, just stood looking at the activity among the spectators as they pestered attendants to show them where their seats were. Amid the hustle and bustle, bookies' runners darted up and down the aisles taking bets on the forthcoming fights. Most punters waited until the fighters climbed into the ring to note their condition before placing bets.

I stood and looked in amazement at the miz maz going on. During all my years as a boxer I'd spent most of my time in the dressing rooms so now my curiosity made me study the form.

Suddenly I felt a hand on my arm and turned to see top boxing manager, Terry Lawless who managed Frank Bruno and other top boxers. Terry, one of the gentlemen of boxing, leaned close to me and said, 'Smile, for your boy's sake, smile.'

I must have been looking really worried and I don't know why but I felt much relieved after hearing those few words of advice. Yes, of course, Terry was right. If I looked worried then Wall would also be worried. I walked back into the dressing room all smiles.

Joe was preparing a bag of cotton buds, Vaseline, adrenaline and other concoctions ready to take to the corner while John was moving around the dressing room warming up. But I was worried, as I thought about how the Londoners would try and secure a win for their new star boy. I knew they didn't rate Wall too highly and had prepared themselves for another win, and they were probably under the impression they had the ref on their side. The dressing room door opened and an official looked inside and asked, 'Wall, ready?'

I gave a nod. This was the moment of truth. 'Ready?' I asked, looking my boxer squarely in the eyes.

'Yea,' was his curt reply.

'Let's go then,' I said and walked out of the door followed by Wall with Joe at the rear. We walked down the corridor, past men who wished Wall the best of luck. Mark Bliss came behind us with his entourage. I imagined that they also wished him luck. We entered the hall to the thunderous roar of the crowd, among them the Welsh supporters. I knew by the shouts of, 'John Wall,' that he wasn't alone in his attempt to win his first pro fight. An official pointed to a corner. I mounted the steps onto the ring apron and held the ropes for Wall to climb through, while Joe remained at the foot of the steps busying himself with bottles of water. I stood in the corner as Wall danced around the ring to the applause of the crowd, then more thunderous applause as Mark Bliss entered the ring.

The ref also climbed into the ring, walked to each corner and looked at the gloves worn by the fighters. Then the MC jumped through the ropes and announced the boxers to the applause of Welsh fans and Cockneys alike. The Cockneys always showed their appreciation of a good fighter. The ref called both fighters to the centre of the ring, gave his instructions and then sent them back to their corners.

The bell sounded to start the first round. The ref waved the boys together and the fight began. I had spent a long time researching Mark Bliss, and discovered he had plenty of stamina and was an all action fighter whose technique was to wear his opponent down. Bliss would attack and make the other man work, keeping the pressure on until through exhaustion, his opponent could no longer defend himself and would collapse, or until the ref stopped the fight.

The crowd who expected an exciting contest wasn't disappointed. Wall, who was also a strong fighter, didn't stand toe to toe with Bliss but instead he counter punched his opponent, catching him as he moved forward, then retaliated with combinations. As each round ended the crowd was getting more and more excited and at the end of the fifth I knew that our Merthyr lad was in front. Wall sat on the corner stool for me to freshen him up in preparation for the sixth and final round and, just as the bell was about to signal the start of the round, I said, 'Now John, you're winning, but you must have a good last round to make sure of the result'. Wall nodded, stood up as the bell sounded and walked to the centre of the ring, touched gloves with Bliss and the last round to decide supremacy between two good fighters started. It seemed a long three minutes before the timekeepers bell signalled the end of the fight and both boys walked to the ref, each expecting his hand to be raised in victory. I could feel my stomach churning with the fear and expectation of a wrong decision being given, but, to my great relief, the ref caught hold of Wall's hand and raised it in the air. Mark Bliss' London fans, appreciating a good winner, joined the Welsh in applauding the decision.

For the first time since arriving in London I could feel my face beaking into a genuine smile. As far as I was concerned, it was a win for John Wall, for Wales and for George's Troedyrhiw boxing gym. We left the ring and walked towards the dressing room with everyone slapping Wall on the back and congratulating him on winning a good fight. My fear of the ref giving an unjust decision had been forgotten. We had the right result and we walked tall. Oh yes, this was the life. John Wall's win meant we were all winners.

John Wall ran up eleven straight wins as featherweight and was steadily climbing the British ratings when fate took a hand and he married his long time girl friend Teresa.

Boxing can put a great strain on married life and there are great demands on the fighter and his family. The wife has to be supportive, prepare the proper food and encourage her husband to eat accordingly. She has to cope with being alone in the evenings while her husband is in the gym training and also cope with the fighter's temperament at home. The strain of trying to adjust to the demands can cause problems and a young, married couple have to pull together to live with the inevitable pressure.

Wall could not control his weight, moved up to lightweight and was still struggling to make the limit. I always thought that at featherweight Wall could have won the British Championship; even so, at lightweight, he was to make a name in boxing by becoming Welsh Lightweight Champion.

Chapter 23

Gym Nights

Back in Merthyr, a typical training night at my Troedyrhiw gym would see my father and Joe sitting in front of a roaring coal fire. That was the meeting place where, on a cold night all would gather around the fire tended by anyone who could get hold of the poker. Joe would be timing the boys skipping, working on punch bags or shadow boxing, while a couple of boys were gloved up waiting for me to arrive before starting to spar. Stepping into the gym, I'd look around and acknowledge the two human fireguards, 'Hello Joe, all right Dad.' A quick chat and I'd walk among the boxers.

'How's your weight, Roy? Did you go for a run this morning, John?'

Joe would look at the clock and say, 'The boys are ready to spar, George.'

'Okay Joe, start them off,' and I'd jump onto the boxing ring apron to watch them sparring.

My father, although now crippled with arthritis, was still mentally sharp. Having been in boxing all his life, he was content to watch the action, give me advice and join in the chatter among old fighters sitting around the fire. Former boxer, Cuthbert Taylor, unable to sit because of his arthritic hips would lean against the side of the ring watching the boys sparring. Cuthbert told how, his hips joints having rotted through arthritis, he was one of the first locally to have hip replacement surgery. He was encased in Plaster of Paris from his neck to his waist for twelve months after the operation. The surgery was never a success and he suffered for the rest of his life. My father also had to have two hip replacements. Former boxers Ben and Tommy Smith, also suffered with arthritic hips and in the early days of surgery had plates put between the joints that were no good at all. They too would join the growing crowd around the vigorously burning fire.

Former boxer Gerry Donovan, who became a councillor and Mayor of Merthyr was a visitor to the gym, and another former boxer, Danny Andrews from Treharris, told of the time he fought and beat Tommy Farr, who boxed from flyweight to heavyweight. The two had met as flyweights and Danny knocked Tommy Farr out.

Nobody gave thought as to why all the old fighters were disabled in some way. Some struggled to walk as their hips, riddled with arthritis gave pain with every step, while others with gnarled knuckles groped awkwardly as they struggled to hold something because continual punching had caused deformity of the knuckle joints. Arm joints were arthritic due to years of punching bags and bodies; knee joints were arthritic and the spine gave severe pain because the wear and tear due to road running and excessive training wore out joints and discs. Old fighters were called 'sleepy eyes' because the continuous cutting of eyebrows had killed the nerves and muscles that held up the eyelids. Young fighters, training hard, didn't think about the effects of a lifetime's boxing, neither did boxing managers nor promoters, doctors nor professional boxing administrators. Nobody gave thought that after retiring, fighters might suffer for their dedication to boxing.

Every so often Joe put coal on the blazing fire to keep the momentum going while my father, poker in hand, would prod away as sparks splattered everywhere. The old time boxers enjoyed watching the sparring before entering into the familiar conversation of old fighters, always about boxing, 'Remember that show in the Merthyr Labour Club with Tommy Farr on the bill, what year was that now? 1930-31?'

The stories bounced around from one old fighter to another as they roasted in front of the fire. Some stories were funny, some solemn and some obviously fictitious but all were educational to an extent.

As the young fighters finished their training many would gather around the fire and listen to the old fighters' yarns. Throughout the evening, men wandered into the gym, some not so interested in watching the boys training as in hearing the conversations and old stories about boxing.

Occasionally, some well dressed chap called into the gym champing an unlit cigar, wondering whether he should light up and risk getting told off for smoking among the boxers (I surely would have told him) or let the cigar hang from his mouth to let others think he was a class above. He would usually walk among the known fighters (old and new) shaking their hands.

There was the newspaper reporter who regularly called to supposedly watch the boys training, until I discovered that all he really wanted was to watch the boys changing and I booted him out.

Occasionally, Joe would stop off at Cardiff fruit market to buy chestnuts that he'd scatter in the ashes under the fire and leave until they split with the heat. Then all were welcome to use the poker and pull them out to eat. When the boxers finished training they would do their floor exercises, put a towel around their shoulders and push in among the scorched gathering to benefit from the heat. Then we'd move one of the tables closer to the warmth where I'd massage any boxer due to box. Massage was an art my father had taught me.

The boxers eager to get home would shower, change their clothes and leave, while those who remained, sitting too close to the fire, carried on listening to the talk of boxing in the old days. They listened to the crackle of the now dying embers, smell the melting tar from the coal, the scorched clothes, wintergreen oil and the dust still floating in the air from being disturbed by the smack of leather skipping ropes on the floorboards.

Wanting to leave myself, I'd ask, 'Right dad, are you ready?'

''Ang on,' he'd say. 'Let me finish this story first,' and I'd have to listen again to one of the stories that I knew by heart. One by one the old timers reluctantly moved from the grate that now contained only the last embers, while Joe tipped water on the remaining sparks to make sure that no fire started after everyone had left. The 'Goodbyes,' and, 'See you tomorrows' were exchanged and another gym night ended.

As one particular gym night came to and end I was trying to persuade my father and Joe to leave the warmth of the fire when the door opened and Eddie Thomas breezed in. He hadn't been seen for some time in boxing circles and was invited to join us by the fire. Eddie asked me if I'd allow him to bring some fighters to train at my gym and explained that a number of boxers had asked him to manage them. Two of these came from Australia. But Eddie wasn't keen on managing run of the mill boxers and was only interested in looking after champions. When the Australian boxers arrived in Wales, they asked me to manage them and Eddie agreed.

Eddie Thomas brought a number of fighters to my gym to train that were self managed or managed by someone else, including former British heavyweight champion Danny McAlindon from Ireland, who was managed by Jack Solomons.

I continued to build up my boxing stable by signing boxers from Cardiff, Swansea, Port Talbot and Merthyr. Paul Boyce, owner of Paul Boyce Auto's, Briton Ferry, asked me to manage him and we became friends.

Meanwhile, two former pro boxers from Merthyr re-entered the boxing scene when Gerald Jones joined my gym as a trainer and Don James who had been granted a manager's licence opened his own gym in Abercanaid and started managing other

Merthyr boxers. In the Bargoed valley Dai Gardner was also granted a manager's licence and once again the South Wales Valleys came alive with pro boxing. And so the boxing business continued, and what a learning process it was with me, on some occasions having to break the rules.

On 15th February, 2004 I arranged for John Wall to fight Martin Galleozzie, another Merthyr fighter, for the Welsh Lightweight Championship over ten rounds at Rhydycar. It was a fairly even match but I knew my man was the stronger and the plan was for my lad to force the pace in order to make his opponent, who was a boxer, fight back. The first round went well with both boxers trying to dominate in front of what was largely a Merthyr crowd. At the end of the first round Wall came back to the corner with blood dripping from a cut that ran the whole length of his lower lip, through which I could see his teeth. Oh hell, what was I going to do to stop the bleeding? It was not in a dangerous position but if it continued the ref might stop the fight. The BBBC's ruling is that corner men are allowed to use 1000-I, strength adrenaline on cuts, to stop the bleeding but the dosage is so weak it rarely does the job properly. Most corner men take two bottles of adrenaline into the corner with them, a bottle of 1000-1 strength to show the boxing board rep' if asked, and a bottle of 100-1, strength to secretly use on cuts should the need arise.

I looked at my boxer's cut and winced, the wound was open like a filleted mackerel. Once the skin has been ripped open it is possible sometimes to stop the bleeding, but nothing can make the skin knit together in such a short period of time. With cotton buds stuck in my top pocket, behind my ears and in my mouth I waited in apprehension for each round to end. John Wall fought like a good-un, sticking to the plan and forcing the fight. To my delight, Galleozzie, instead of using his reach to box, retaliated and fought back. This was exactly what we wanted. He was playing right into out hands. When the bell rang to end the fight it was clear that Wall had done enough to be given the verdict and when the ref raised his arm as winner, the whole crowd went wild. I looked at the cut under Wall's lower lip. It was flapping like another set of lips and I looked at an empty bottle of adrenaline, along with other secret potions. The bleeding had stopped but the boxer would need many stitches to close the wound. However, there were no regrets; my man had won the fight.

Chapter 24

Booth Fighting

Ever looking for new ventures I thought back to times when great Welsh boxers like Jimmy Wilde, Freddie Welsh, Jim Driscoll, Ronnie James, Tom Thomas, Tommy Farr and thousands of others learned their trade in the boxing booths. I decided to re-introduce booth boxing to Wales, and in July 1982 the Brandy Bridge nightclub in Merthyr Tydfil was chosen as my venue. My former boxing manager Mac Williams was contacted and he enrolled former stable mate Tony Bennett.

Once the boxing booth was advertised, the whole of Merthyr and surrounding valleys were buzzing with the news and requests from would be fighters flooded in. The BBC arranged television coverage and newspapers were eager to get reports.
A boxing ring was erected at the Brandy Bridge club, lighting and seating organised, a doctor hired as well as everything else that went with promoting. The show was a sellout, but I had not charged much of an entrance fee and already accepted that after paying a doctor, security, and my own boxers and challengers I would probably end up losing money.

The night of the show arrived and the hall quickly filled up with spectators. It was unlikely that any of the challengers had been in the boxing ring before so I told them not to worry, that the booth fighters knew the score and wouldn't hurt them.

The first fight of the evening was announced between a coal merchant from Merthyr and one of my boxers. The bell rang to start the first round and the coal merchant, eager to please the audience, rushed at the boxer and started slugging away left and right, not realizing that his punches were having little effect because they landed on the boxer's arms. The crowd warmed to the spectacle and shouted for the underdog, willing him on. Not to be outdone, the boxer retaliated with some stiff jabs but purposely didn't follow up, thus allowing the coal merchant to exchange leather. The sound of the bell brought a roar of approval from the audience that only ebbed slightly during the minute interval, before starting again in round two when the pugilists exchanged leather again. There was one more round between my boxer and the coal merchant who was overjoyed at having fought three rounds in public for the first time in his life. It was a tremendous night, nobody got hurt but scores of young lads wanted to know when the next show would be held, wanting to have their go in the booth.

Throughout the following week, I was inundated with phone calls from organisations across Wales wanting me to run a boxing booth for them. Then the bomb dropped. The Welsh Area Council of the British Boxing Board of Control summoned Mac and me to attend a meeting. Although booth boxing wasn't illegal, it had been banned by the Boxing Board and we were ticked off and fined two hundred pounds each.

My own feeling was that since there was such a huge response by would-be boxers and spectators, had booth boxing been allowed to continue under strict controls it would have revitalised the flagging world of professional boxing. But that was it, the end of booth boxing in Merthyr Tydfil, before it had a chance to become established.

I was still ducking and diving, looking to earn a pound or two when, from an idea I'd been given I invented a self-supporting boxing ring that could be erected by one person in less than twenty minutes. The ring had four wooden corner posts each standing in hollow steel supports. Running from each corner post were lengths of steel supports. Three ropes hanging from hooks in the corner posts provided the square ring that supported itself. I erected the ring on the mountainside above Troedyrhiw and invited the *South Wales Echo* to witness the event. My intention was to take out a patent and register my invention, but the cost of this, considering the few who would require a self-supporting boxing ring, didn't make it a viable proposition.

At this time I was being approached by other boxing people with regards to promoting boxing shows locally, but I declined the offer because it involved charities in what can only be described as a con. It was put to me that the easiest way to promote a boxing show and make a lot of money was to involve some kind of charitable organization which would provide people to work and sell tickets. After the show, only the promoter really knew how much money was made. A certain amount of the profit could be handed to the charity to keep them happy and the promoter kept the biggest share. I wanted no part of it.

Of all the places I visited in connection with boxing I favoured London during the 60s, 70s and 80s when I spent a lot of time in the city. I liked the razmataz and the excitement that came from Soho, Chinatown, and all the other West and East End areas where I would visit restaurants, pubs, clubs, and business premises. For a lad out of Merthyr it was exciting and I was enjoying the experience. My visit to Solomons' office would be welcomed by the customary smile from Jack and an invitation to help myself at the drinks cabinet. My polite refusal would be met with Solomons' gorgeous mini skirted secretary pouring me a glass of brandy and offering to 'look after me.' But I already knew of boxing managers who had fallen into that tender trap and subsequently into the promoter's pocket.

Being in the company of well-known personalities usually meant I would down three or four large drinks before leaving

Solomons' office. There was no breathalyzer test in those days and drinking during the day was regarded by some as acceptable.

Visits to London became a regular thing. On one occasion with Joe in tow, and wearing my recently purchased green velvet jacket, light green open necked shirt and matching trousers, I drove my pink Mercedes to Carnaby Street in the West End where we had arranged to meet two friends, Jim and Phil. After a visit to a pub we were walking through Soho laughing and joking as was the norm after a few drinks, when, as usual, I was led astray and dragged into a pub that had a disco in the cellar. We walked through the door and down some steps into the cellar disco. Joe went in first, turned around and came back out.

'Jesus,' he said, 'you can't see your hand in front of your face in there.' It wasn't so much dark, although the lighting was dim, as thick with cigarette smoke.

The place was packed with all sorts and all colours and this was during the afternoon. We found a table but had to share it with two women, both about forty years old, who were dressed in long flowery dresses, had long auburn hair and wore thick makeup on their wrinkled faces.

The disco sound was booming and the lights flashing. I shouted to Joe, 'Keep your eye on the time, I need to go over to the Strand about ten.' It was quite usual for me to leave London and head for home at about 4 am, arrive back in Merthyr at about 6.30 am and snatch one hour's sleep before going to the steelworks. I looked at the six of us sitting around the table. Jim, forty plus years old was tall and thin with long black hair. He wore a yellow two-piece suit with bell bottom trousers and brown suede shoes. He was trying to sing. He'd been chewing dope and was as high as a kite. Phil, also in his forties, of average build with short greying hair wore black slacks and a black shortie mac. Phil, who never took the mac off, had closed his eyes and was trying to sleep! How the hell he could even try to doze with the disco banging away was beyond belief.

Joe, who wore his usual fawn trousers and matching cardigan, kept puffing on his fag and swilling beer, and asking, 'When was the Great Wall of China built?' Good old Joe.

The two women were rolling joints when all of a sudden one of them climbed onto the table and started dancing.

We'd been in the disco for about an hour. You couldn't hear for the noise and you couldn't see for the smoke. Then, suddenly, all hell broke loose when a bloke standing against the wall walked over to a young boy leaning against the bar and butted him in the ear.

'Aaah!' The unfortunate youth held his ear, face twisted in agony.

It was as if the butt was a signal, because people started fighting all around with bodies rolling all over the floor. Without warning a young black chap picked up a set of disco lights and smashed them into Jim's face and blood spurted everywhere, covering one of the women sitting next to him. Without even thinking, I retaliated and hit the guy who by this time was lashing out at everybody within striking distance. I then looked at my hand and saw two front teeth sticking out of the knuckle! There was blood everywhere and pandemonium as other revellers felt like joining in the bash. The police were called and within minutes were swarming all over the place walloping everybody with batons.

Then an ambulance arrived and two ambulance men carrying a stretcher ran into the room. Seeing the woman covered in blood they picked her up, put her on the stretcher, ran back to the ambulance and with sirens going sped off to hospital. The woman on the stretcher, having smoked enough dope to flatten a camel, quietly went along with their action.

Jim, was holding a blood soaked hanky to his nose that was split in two. Joe and I lifted our injured companion and tried to persuade a copper that my pal needed an ambulance. 'Hold on there,' said the policeman, 'I need to take a statement from you.'

As the copper walked away (I assume to get a note book), Phil came to life rubbing his eyes and the three of us dragged the unfortunate Jim out of the pub. I had no idea what the time was. It was dark now and my intention was to get my injured companion to a hospital. The four of us, being well oiled, were staggering through the streets of Soho, three of us splitting our sides laughing while Jim kept singing. It was more of a gurgling as he held a hanky to his nose. Joe and I were well used to facial cuts and split noses, so we weren't too bothered, Evn so it didn't need a doctor to see that Jim needed medical treatment. Oddly enough, passers by didn't seem in the least bit interested. At last we managed to stop a taxi but as we started to climb in the driver said, 'Hang on mate, you'd better not get any blood on my motor.'

Eventually, we arrived at a hospital, and it was as we climbed out of the taxi that I could see that my green clothes were now dark red from Jim's blood. Leaving Jim to the mercy of a doctor who spoke poor English, and a nurse who picked up a needle about the size of a knitting needle we headed home, where I had to bin my new set of clothes.

There were times when I was taking one of my boxers to a show when his family or friends would ask if they could tag along. On one such outing to London, when one of my fighters was boxing at the NSC, Clive Evans, a mate travelled with us. After the weigh-in we had lunch and I booked the fighter into the Regent's Palace hotel where he rested for the afternoon. The rest of us decided to spend a few hours around the West End. There were eight of us walking through Soho when a spiv approached and asked us if we wanted to see a striptease. I tried telling the lads that it was only a rip off, but being new to that area of London, the others wanted to see the show so I collected the three pounds entrance fee from each of the other chaps and handed it to the spiv.

'Right lads,' he said, 'follow me.' We walked behind him along the streets of Soho finally stopping outside a club. 'In here,' said our guide and we followed him through a doorway, along a corridor and across a room, through another door and found ourselves back out on the streets with no sign of the swine we'd given the money to!

Back in Merthyr, John Wall had acquired a big following and seeing his potential as a draw, Eddie Thomas started to run shows at Rhydycar Leisure Centre.

All the boxing shows at Rhydycar with John Wall topping the bill were sell-outs, and as Wall's manager it was my duty to try and make as much money as possible for my boxer. After one of the shows I approached Eddie Thomas and told him that for any future shows with Wall on I wanted a percentage of the gate on top of his purse. Eddie looked sheepish and said, 'George, you will have to see Jack Solomons. He's the governor. It's his show and his money.' Suddenly everything dropped into place and all the puzzling bits and pieces became clear when I realised that Solomons was doing all the say-so.

Shortly after that conversation with Eddie I travelled to a boxing show at the Grosvenor House Hotel, Park Lane, and attended the weigh-in. Jack Solomons approached me and offered me a deal. Arrangements between top promoters and managers are fairly common when a good fighter comes on the scene and the promoter helps by matching the fighter on his shows. But Solomons wanted me to let him have full control over all my boxers so that he could match them as he pleased. If I required a contest for one of my boxers involving another promoter then I would have to ask Solomons first. Also, I was not allowed to ask what my fighters were getting paid before a contest. If a boxer wanted to know how much he was being paid for a fight, I was to tell him he would find out after he had fought. Solomons told me that way he would give us more. He then told me that that was how he did business with Eddie Thomas and confirming what Eddie had told me in Rhydycar. I then understood why some of Eddie's boxers didn't know how much they were being paid before each fight.

I thought long and hard about the offer. If Solomons had full control over my boxing stable, some of my boys might have good matches, but I considered myself a good manager. However, Solomons had guided other boxers, but how much money had they made out of boxing? The impression was that Eddie would drop out of boxing altogether. It became clear to me that Solomons wanted me to take Eddie's place and be guided by the London promoter. Then I thought about my other boxers and how they would be treated. Would they be used as fodder for Solomons' shows and would they have to fight for peanuts?

The syndicate was the big gun in British boxing promotions but there was a new face on the scene. Frank Warren had started promoting and the word was that he had massive financial support behind him and was likely to be the top in boxing in a couple of years. I decided that it would be better all round if I stayed as I was.

Chapter 25

Winston Allen

One of the most charismatic boxers I ever managed was Cardiff's black heavyweight, Winston Allen, whom I first met on a visit to the Swansea boxing gym where he trained. Managed by a Swansea man, Allen trained in an upstairs room of a building next to Swansea prison. Upon entering the gym I was faced with the bizarre scene where half was a boxing gym, another part a poolroom and yet another part, a massage/beauty parlor. How anyone could concentrate on training while young girls wearing bikinis wandered around is anybody's guess!

The fit looking heavyweight had fought eleven contests and won most of them. His punching power was impressive. But I noticed that Allen wasn't training properly. He would skip for a while then stop and walk into the next room to talk to the girls. He'd then punch the bag for a while. In fact, Allen did exactly what he wanted which wasn't much. He was a big strong man who had a hefty punch in both fists and I realised that if he trained properly he could become one hell of a good fighter. During a conversation Allen told me that he wasn't happy with his current management so I bought his contract.

Winston Allen and I hit it off from the start. He was a likable, woman loving character who was always looking for fun. My new heavyweight did his basic training in Cardiff and a month before each fight he lived in Merthyr where I trained him. Allen got off to a good start and after a couple of fights under my management he was doing well.

I was sitting in my office when a phone call came through from Allen, whom I hadn't heard from since his last fight about two months previously.

'Boss, I'm skint,' he said over the phone. 'Can you get me a fight?'

I spent the rest of the week checking with agents and promoters at home and abroad and finely accepted a match against the Belgian heavyweight boxer, Jean Pierre Coopman, to be staged in Belgium. Then began negotiations over purse money, expenses and the flight from Heathrow to Belgium. My request for two single rooms with en-suite for Winston and me at a first class hotel was agreed.

I did some research which included watching a film of Coopman boxing, and noticed that he continually dropped his right hand. The trouble was that although Allen had one hell of a punch, he couldn't throw a left hook. Winston Allen would have to end the fight quickly because if it went the distance, it was odds on that Coopman would have a hometown decision. I made a special hook and jab pad to get Winston to throw a good left hook, feeling that that was the tool for the job and after a month's hard training he was ready.

A flight was booked from Heathrow and at the massive air terminal we eventually found our departure point, checked our luggage and then decided to have a meal. Finally, it was time to catch our flight and we were taken by bus across the runway. During the short ride I looked at the two other people on board and wondered where all the other passengers were. The bus stopped, we climbed off and I looked around. Where was the aircraft? We were led to the Belgian flight which to my horror was an eight-seat charter plane. We crouched low in order to board and I looked around. Where was the hostess to show us to our seats and point out the emergency and safety points?

There wasn't one! They could, at least, have given us parachutes!

Okay, so where do we put our luggage? 'On your lap,' was the answer to that question. 'No, not on the floor or it will fly around. Hold your luggage on your lap.'

Winston and I looked at each other, both feeling rather apprehensive. Then a bloke climbed aboard wearing an uniform. He sat in the cockpit, so he must have been the pilot. As he sat by the controls, a woman, also wearing an uniform, came on board and sat next to him. We suddenly realised that she was the pilot.

Like many people at that time I had travelled by aeroplane but always in one of the large variety. I'd never been in such a small aircraft, I was seated so close to the pilot I could touch her on the shoulder. Winston and I both agreed that we'd prefer to go through the buildup to a fight to riding in a small areoplane like that one.

The flight to Belgium was memorable to say the least. The plane frequently dropped leaving one's stomach in the air. The final fright of the journey was when it suddenly nose-dived towards earth for landing. Safely on the ground, we left the plane and walked on wobbly legs through the airport where a man approached us. He introduced himself as our guide and took us for a meal. When we'd finished eating he took us by car to our hotel. The opposition usually tries to upset the opponent and there was no exception on this occasion. At a second class hotel, Allen and I had been booked into the same room containing two single beds, two bedside cabinets, a wardrobe and a washbasin in the corner. There was little in the way of welcome.

The show was to be held on the following day. We attended the weigh in and press conference before going for a meal, then, after lunch, we went to the hotel for Winston to rest. The evening soon came around. A car arrived to take us to the venue and we were shown into a dressing room that was small, ill furnished and had no running water or washing facilities. I went to see the promoter who, when I asked him for a different dressing room, said 'Not possible.' I started arguing but the promoter turned to the men with him and conducted the usual ploy of speaking Flemish, totally ignoring me. I found the agent who told me to go back to our dressing room while he confronted the promoter. Winston Allen knew nothing of the disagreement, it was better for him to think that everything was okay. Eventullay the agent came to say that we would have to keep the same dressing room, but a shower and washing facilities would be provided. I was content with that. I insisted on seeing a boxing official and demanded to be allowed to watch Coopman being bandaged. 'Not possible. That's my job,' he said.

I bandaged and taped Allen's hands. He changed into his boxing gear and I greased him. Winston was fighting top of the bill and after a couple of preliminary bouts the whip called for us. Before leaving for the arena I took two bottles from my bag, nipped into a room where there was a tap and filled them with water. There were always bottles of water in the corners, but how did we know what had been put in them?

The boxing hall was packed full of Coopman's fans, all shouting his name and I was hoping that Winston Allen wouldn't freeze. When I got to the corner, I put the bottles of water on the floor. The corner assistant started to object, and pointed to the bottles of water already there. He shook his head as he looked at the bottles I put there. He turned as if to call someone. I kicked the two other bottles under the ring and picked mine up. I shook my head making it plain that I wanted to use the water I had brought. The corner assistant eventually shrugged his shoulders in resignation. Changing the water bottles may not have made a difference, but on the other hand it could have?

Winston climbed into the ring and both boxers were announced while Coopman's fans kept shouting his name, stamping their feet and booing Winston. The bell sounded and the fight began. The first round went quietly enough as both men felt their way around, but in the second round Coopman had come out of his corner to start in earnest when suddenly, Winston Allen crashed a left hook against his jaw and he dropped to the floor, out cold. In realizing that Winston Allen had won the fight the Coopman fans went quiet. There were a few people who clapped as the decision was announced but, not surprisingly, no congratulations from the promoter, not that we cared.

Ah well, another day, another dollar, as they say. Then another hair-raising flight back home.

Twelve months after signing with me Winston Allen had chalked up a number of KO wins and I decided to take a chance and accept a fight in Bilbao, against the Spanish Heavyweight Champion Alfredo Evangelista. It was well known in the boxing world that it was almost impossible to get a win in Spain, but having been offered a big purse it was worth taking a puncher's chance. If Winston lost on points nobody would have thought any the less of him for losing in Spain and he would have gained a lot of big fight experience and earned good money.

Also well known in the boxing world was how difficult it was to get paid by the Spaniards after the fight. So, before we left Britain I negotiated over the telephone with the Spaniards and insisted that I'd only take the fight on condition that we'd be paid cash in sterling the same night.

We flew from Heathrow and arrived in Barcelona to a fairly cold reception; no problem, we hadn't been expecting any different. We'd been booked into a hotel where we rested, then spent some time looking around the Spanish city. The following day, we attended the weigh-in, then had a light lunch before going back to the hotel for Winston to rest before the evening show. The fight went well for Winston Allen. He fought ten good rounds but as expected didn't get the decision. After the fight Winston had a shower and got changed while I went to see the promoter for the fight money. I knocked at the office door and was admitted by a hefty looking character. I could see the promoter and a couple of blokes having a bit of chit-chat. The promoter handed me a cheque for the purse money, which I refused, reminding him of our agreement. After a lengthy discussion in Spanish they offered me a cheque for part of the payment and pesetas to make up the difference, but I refused again and there followed an argument. 'We don't have enough cash,' they kept insisting and I began to wonder if they were going to tuck us up. The promoter began thumping the table and shouting in Spanish, undoubtedly trying to intimidate. But each time he thumped the table and shouted, I thumped the table and shook my head. The promoter suddenly stopped shouting and produced a case of cash. I finally accepted part pesetas, part dollars and part sterling in cash. It turned out we had lost about thirty pounds on exchange rates but I was content with that.

The following morning we left the hotel for the airport.

Chapter 26

Boxing Changes

John Wall, having won the Welsh Lightweight Championship prepared for his first defence against local boxer Billy Vivian.

Heddwyn Taylor, one of the small Welsh promoters prepared to gamble his money was promoting the show at Ebbw Vale, home of the Steel works on the 13th July, 1977.

The problem was that John Wall was having difficulty keeping to the lightweight limit of nine stone nine pounds. The night before the contest I took him to my gym and checked his weight. Wall stepped onto the scale and came in one pound over the limit.

'Okay John,' I said, 'That'll do nicely, nothing to eat or drink now or tomorrow and you'll come in well under the limit.'

Unfortunately John couldn't resist eating snacks.

The day of the show we travelled to Ebbw Vale Leisure Centre and attended the weigh-in. Heddwyn Taylor was there; Billy Vivian and his manager Dai Gardner were there as were all the other fighters on the show and their managers. The Boxing Board of Control arrived to officiate and the doctor attended. The atmosphere was thick with boxing. Everyone talked boxing. Then, as the fighters were getting changed ready to be weighed Heddwyn Taylor suddenly cried out, 'Oh no, I've forgotten to hire a weighing machine.'

The talking stopped when the realization of what Heddwyn had said struck home. According to the Boxing Board of Control, weighing scales must be hired for the weigh-in, checked and certified correct, at every boxing show.

Then Heddwyn broke the silence when he announced, 'It's alright there's a scale in the foyer.'

He ran out into the foyer and stood by the public weighing scales searching his pockets for coins to make it work. All present followed in disbelief. 'Right, who's first,' shouted Heddwyn. To this day, I don't know how the Board's Official allowed it to happen because no one knew if the scale was weighing correctly. Dai Gardner was shaking his head and the Boxing Boards reps were scratching their heads wondering what to do. Billy Vivian stepped onto the scales. Heddwyn put a coin in the slot and the needle swung around, stopping just below the lightweight limit of nine stone nine pounds. Vivian stepped off the scale and John Wall took his place as Heddwyn put another coin in the slot. The needle swung around the clock past nine stone nine pounds. I was amazed and asked myself how Wall was overweight, but of course he must have eaten since I had weighed him the previous night.

Dai Gardner reminded all present, 'If Wall can't make the weight the fight can't be for the title.'

John Wall stepped off the scales but I encouraged him back on and said, 'Let him try again.'

As soon as the needle reached nine stone nine pounds I pulled him off the scales and said, 'That's it, nine stone, nine pounds,' and I could see the Board Official writing nine stone, nine pounds on the form.

Dai Gardner was shaking his head again. The Board rep shrugged his shoulders and Heddwyn Taylor was trying to rush everyone out of the foyer. That night John Wall beat Billy Vivian on points.

It was business as usual one night at my gym when young boxer Johnny Owen and his father, Dick, arrived. Dick, who did all the talking, asked me if Johnny could train at my gym and I agreed. I remembered Johnny when, as a young lad, he first began boxing with my father at the Plymouth Street Boxing Club. Johnny was a quiet lad who came to the gym and got on with his work. After many months at my gym, Johnny was thinking of turning professional and he and his father asked what I thought about managing him. I'd watched Johnny boxing in his last two amateur contests and hadn't been impressed because he'd taken a lot of stick and was well beaten on both counts. With this in mind, I didn't encourage him, but I had reckoned without his commitment to training and the durability, which enabled him to become a champion.

Dick Owen then took Johnny to manager Dai Gardner, who worked with boxing promoter Heddwyn Taylor. At least Johnny Owen can be thankful for Heddwyn Taylor's efforts in arranging suitable matches for him.

'Bagful of monkeys,' Les Roberts, matchmaker of the National Sporting Club had been successful in Welsh boxing for many years and had made a lot of money by using the NSC promoter's licence to run shows in Wales. Les kept an eye on Welsh boxers and when he saw a likely prospect used his influence as matchmaker of the NSC to become agent for the latest attraction. When young Johnny Owen started winning his early pro contests, Les could see an opening.

Owen went from strength to strength. Although not a hard hitter he was fit and strong and had the ability to wear an opponent down.

When Johnny turned pro he tightened his defence by using his arms and gloves as a shield. He still took punishment that many an opponent would have succumbed to, but Johnny's body belied his stubborn will, determination and courage. He went on to become British, Commonwealth and European champion. Johnny was not an exciting fighter to watch, he didn't have the talent or charisma of Howard Winstone, thus he didn't encourage a following from the valleys. It was only in death that his heroism was fully celebrated.

After losing only one of his twenty-six professional contests Johnny challenged Mexican Lupe Pintor for his world bantamweight title at the Olympic Auditorium in Los Angeles on the 19th September, 1980. Many people thought that he was taking on too much by challenging the tough Mexican with a record of forty-one victories and seven defeats. But by being triple champion Johnny deserved his chance. Unfortunately there was a defect in Johnny's structure that was to put an abrupt end to his young life. His frail skull could not survive Pintor's vicious punches, nor the twelfth and last round of a hard contest. Johnny was ahead on points until halfway through the fight when he began to wilt. Then, with just forty seconds to go a short right hand punch sent Johnny to his knees. After a mandatory count he rose to his feet and was driven across the ring where Pintor gave him a savage right hand punch that sent him backwards and his head hit the floor. Johnny was taken to hospital in a coma where he died seven weeks later.

The boxing scene was on the change. Londoner Frank Warren was taking over. Jack Solomons had died and the syndicate disbanded. Eddie Thomas found the future champion he'd been looking for and signed Colin Jones who trained in my Troedyrhiw gym. Eddie then engaged a London agent to match Colin for him.

The convenience of mobile phones and motorways appeared. Young boxers no longer had to accept local managers but could travel to London and be managed by top promoters, who didn't want the less talented boxers. The ordinary, run of the mill boxers had to be content to accept a local manager who sometimes had difficulty matching his fighters. The result was that six round boxers or boxers who hadn't made the grade were being overmatched since that was the only way they could get fights.

It has been said that boxing managers do not make champions but that champions make managers. In reality, boxers and managers need each other. The true test of a manager comes when he has to build up a run of the mill boxer. That is the reason why many top managers will only look after top fighters and very often when the champion goes, the manager has no option but to go with him.

On the other hand, a manager could work hard for three years building a boxer's career only for the boxer to be poached by another manager. This possibility meant that some managers signed a boxer, not really caring if he eventually made the grade but just matching him for the most money. Despite this way of managing, a boxer will sometimes be good enough to come through and be a champion but with no credit to the manager.

I have met a lot of genuine people in the world of boxing. The majority of boxers I managed were honest workmen who enjoyed the game, enjoyed the money and were grateful for any help I gave them. I also had the misfortune to meet the bums that sneaked into boxing. Also there were the fathers who did nothing but moan and groan, were never an asset to their son's boxing careers and just ended up making the scene miserable.

There are the promoters who think nothing of having some new young boxer knocked off to make a good fight on their show, ruining the boxer's career in the process. There might also be referees who are tied with promoters into giving bad decisions thus stopping young hopefuls from realising their ambitions.

And yet, despite all the downs relating to boxing there are also many ups. You meet the gentlemen of boxing, many of whom work in the sport for nothing. They just enjoy seeing boxers succeed in the game. There are the top boxing men who make the money, but there are small promoters who always lose money and these are the ones who must be helped because without them boxing as we know it will cease.

Knowing the genuine people, having one of your boxers win a contest, experiencing the smell of sweat mixed with wintergreen oil and dust as the boxers train, the coal fire burning in the gym was the magic that kept me in the game for all those years.

In October 1981 my father died. My mentor in the boxing world, I suppose my father was the person I moulded myself on. He was the one I could always rely on for sensible advice, even though many times I thought I knew best but found out later I hadn't. My father was a wise man who had the knack of 'weighing someone up' quickly. He had a way of telling a story that made it interesting and he had short sayings that spoke volumes. If he thought I was getting involved with an untrustworthy character he'd say, 'Watch him George, he's like a bagful of monkeys.'

When my father died, for me the flame of boxing diminished; it wasn't the same anymore.

Chapter 27

Back at Guest Keen

Back at Dowlais Steel Works (it should have been called Butlins holiday camp) Gilbert James retired early, Derlwyn Kent became cashier and I was promoted to chief wages clerk. A couple of years later Derlwyn accepted early redundancy and I became works cashier. While I was works cashier and chief wages clerk, timekeeper Bryn Williams moved into the wages office under my supervision, until he took redundancy and I was given his work to do as well. There were now only two of us left to run the wages, cashiers and timekeepers and for the first time in a long while I was again working a full week.

My boxing business was thriving, as was Hilary's shop and a number of years passed with me as works cashier and doing very well, thank you very much.

On my visits to cities I'd buy cheap gear like watches and clothes and then drive into work, open the car boot and start flogging my wares to the office staff. This often included fruit and vegetables left over in the shop. I had to dump them somewhere! I wasn't worried about the works manager objecting. My concern was that he might expect me to give him a percentage of what I earned! Then, on top of what I was already doing, I was asked to collect debts for the company.

This was another excuse for me to leave the works and call into the wholesale warehouses to buy stock for the shop.

It was the life of Reilly, working for British Steel. A contact of mine at Hamiltons Steelworks Cardiff (a subsidiary of British Steel), would phone me. 'Hello George, when can you come down to Cardiff then, I need you to look at some forms.' 'What forms?'

'Oh! I don't know. I'll find some by the time you get down.'

I'd first get permission, then arrange expenses for travelling to Cardiff where I would meet my contact (I often wondered who had the best job, him or me). We'd lunch in Cardiff and discuss some aspect of boxing (very important to British Steel) then I'd travel back to the Dowlais works and find out if anybody from the world of boxing had phoned me, before collecting my expenses.

The expenses lark was rampant among staff workers, especially the senior staff who turned it into a nice little earner. As soon as it was rumoured that the works might be about to close the expense claims increased.

Although busy at the steel works and at Hilary's shop, I still had my boxing business to take care of and Paddy Burns, matchmaker for Irish promoter Barnie Eastwood, rang me and we fixed a match between my boxer Mick Rowley and Peter Eubanks on a show at the Kings Hall, Belfast on the 9th September, 1982 with Barry McGuigan topping the bill. A good payday was agreed for Rowley and Paddy confirmed that he'd booked a flight for us both from Heathrow to Belfast with the tickets to be collected at Heathrow airport. Paddy also booked us both into the Europa Hotel, that was near the Kings Hall.

Rowley was to fly to Belfast at the weekend while I conducted some business in London and then follow him on the day of the fight. Unfortunately, it was at a time when the IRA were exploding bombs everywhere making any trip to Belfast nerve wracking. I drove Rowley to the airport and watched him board the plane before going into London where I'd arranged to spend the weekend. On Monday morning as I left London and drove to Heathrow the sun was shining, the fight arranged for Rowley was a good match. I felt he could win and I was in a good mood.

Heathrow was as busy as usual. I went to collect my flight ticket, only to be told that a seat hadn't been booked for me. I tried to make a booking myself but all the seats on the only flight to Belfast that day were fully booked. I was fuming, Rowley was in Belfast and I was left stranded in London. I was in a sweat. How the hell was I going to get to Belfast? Sure, they would look after Rowley for me and in fact treat him well. Rowley, who was used to travelling and boxing alone in Australia, would have no problem, but what an idiot I felt.

I rang Rowley at the Europa Hotel. 'Yes, George,' he said, 'No problem, they're looking after me. If you can't make it, don't worry.'

But I did worry.

I was rushing around the airport pestering people when suddenly I had a bit of luck. One of the passengers flying to Belfast cancelled and I took the seat. Breathing a huge sigh of relief, I climbed aboard the aircraft but I was still in one hell of a temper. I didn't know what to expect at Belfast Airport, never having been there before, and on landing was surprised to find it almost deserted with no taxis waiting for passengers. I collected my gear and walked around looking for a means of transport to Belfast when a chap wearing a flat cap came over to me and said, 'You looking for a ride, are you then?'

I felt relieved. 'Yes I am,' I answered, 'Are you a taxi driver?'

'I am that to be sure,' he said, 'Follow me,' and he led the way to an old banger that I thought surely couldn't be a taxi.

'Jump in will you now,' said the fellow. I threw my bag into the back of the car and sat next to it.

With a roar of the engine we sped along lanes that seemed to be heading out into the country. On and on we drove for miles with no sign of dwellings or life and I thought back to the previous week when someone had been picked up in Northern Ireland, taken somewhere quiet and murdered. Bloody hell, I thought to myself, this guy is in the IRA and he's going to take me somewhere and shoot me. For a minute I froze, then quickly looked around the car for something to hit the driver with. There was nothing suitable. It's funny how your mind works in such situations and I started talking to the driver. 'I'm Welsh,' I said, just in case he couldn't tell by my accent.

'Oh yea, are you that now.'

'I'm here for the boxing, I've got a fighter on the same bill as McGuigan.'

Surely he wouldn't be interested in killing a Welshman? Then I started to plan what I'd do in an emergency. If the driver slowed down as if intending to stop I'd reach from behind and strangle him. I wonder what that taxi driver would have said if he'd known what I was thinking!

I thought about Paddy Burns safe and sound in the hotel. If only I could live long enough to get hold of him. After a long, tortuous drive through narrow roads I was relieved to see the outline of buildings and finally we reached Belfast and the hotel.

What with me being left high and dry in London and the taxi ride from Belfast Airport, I was in a real state. I paid the driver, walked straight into the hotel and asked the receptionist for Paddy Burns' room number.

To say that Paddy was surprised to see me when he answered the door wearing his underpants and vest is an understatement. I pushed myself into the room. 'Right, you bastard you're for it,' I shouted and chased Paddy back and fore around the table while he kept saying, 'It wasn't me, George, it wasn't me, I didn't do it.'

After what seemed like an hour but could only have been a minute I stopped long enough for Paddy to blurt out his excuse (or Blarney, good old Paddy). It would appear that Paddy had given instructions to an associate (no name) to order two flight tickets. The plonker (he said) had made a mistake. I think it must have been the sight of Paddy striding before me looking ridiculous in his pants and vest that made me shake his outstretched hand. I left the room, still pals with the matchmaker. In fact, once I'd found Mick Rowley I could see that a double room had been booked for us. My boxer was happy (as Mick always was) and we went to the weigh in, had a light lunch and walked around some of the shops in Belfast. We were resting in our room during the afternoon when suddenly there was a knock on the door and boxing manager Billy May from Newport, South Wales, arrived with Sammy Sims, one of his fighters who later became British Featherweight Champion. They wanted to sleep on the floor of our room to avoid having to pay for their own room. No problem with that and both Mick and I agreed.

That night Mick Rowley lost on points to Peter Eubanks.

We arrived back at the hotel and went to our room where we were lying on our beds, when suddenly Billy May and Sammy entered.

'We're going for a drink,' said Billy. 'Leave the door open for us we'll be back in the early hours.'

I thought about all the trouble in Belfast and wondered about leaving the door open, but it was either that or waking up to let them in. We left the door open.

From Ireland it was straight back to the Dowlais works. After a number of senior staff had left the Steel Works, John Owens became manager. John who was about five foot eight inches tall, sort of stocky with a round face tried desperately to stop the works from closing. His whole life seemed to revolve around the Ivor Works. Although redundancies were being offered, many employees kept their heads in the sand and refused to believe that the steelworks would close. Realistically however, closure seemed imminent. The employees all hoped that the next to go would be someone else, not them. Staff workers sat at their desks, afraid to look up in case a redundancy notice was put in front of them.

Most of the workforce at the Ivor were like me and had only ever worked at Dowlais Steel Works and were under the impression that most other companies were the same.

Some office workers on realising that perhaps they might be made redundant began pinching whatever they could lay their hands on. One office secretary waited for the other staff to go to lunch each day then wandered around the offices nicking everything she thought useful.

The other staff workers helped themselves in the same way and if something wasn't screwed down, it soon went missing. Pens, pencils, reams of paper – they all went walkies! In the end, people walked around with their pockets bulging. You didn't know if they had stolen the stuff or if it belonged to them and they were afraid to put anything down.

Out in the works, you couldn't describe the atmosphere as being happy and with good reason. Men were worried about losing their jobs. As for me, I worked lots of overtime and got paid good money. Being my own boss so to speak, and having previously arranged to take holidays when I needed time off, I was still able to travel with the boxing, and as a result I ended up having more holidays than the Queen.

The year of 1982 was coming to an end. Times had been sweet for all at Dowlais steel works and John Owens felt that if every man pulled his finger out and worked hard each shift, the works could still become the best. But it wasn't going to be easy to change a work pattern that had become a tradition. Back in the 1970's, once the workmen had been paid their wages in cash on a Friday, it was customary for them to walk out of the foundry via the back entrance and spend the rest of the day in Dowlais pubs.

The Personnel Manager decided to put a stop to the practice and along with the timekeeper went into every pub in Dowlais ordering the men back to work. But he did not have the co-operation of the foremen and the practice of nipping out of work early was to continue. John Owens wanted to put the responsibility firmly on my shoulders and asked me to control the workers' timekeeping, and make sure that every man paid a full shift was at least in work to earn it.

This request from the Works' Manager wasn't going to be easy for me to carry out since I'd spent years working the same system myself. As I understood it, Dowlais Steel Works was already making a good annual profit so, would saving a couple of minutes working time matter? Besides, surely it was the foremen who would know whether the men were at their jobs or not?

I started to check the whole clocking system and what I discovered was unbelievable, because there were all kinds of cons. In some areas where two men worked together one man clocked in two cards while the other man stayed at home. Maintenance men would take camp beds into work and one was overheard telling his wife, 'I'll go into work early tonight, love, to have a good night's sleep.' It wasn't unusual for a foreman to stumble upon a workman sleeping in one of the moulds during the day.

I'd call to see John Owens to discuss the latest details with him. He thought the workers who were on the fiddle were extremely naïve, and at one point, while stamping around his office smoking a big cigar and looking like Groucho Marx he warned, 'The stupid bastards! Don't they realise what they are doing? They are too thick to understand that they will end up closing the works.'

Although they produced general castings worldwide, Dowlais steel works mainly provided ingots, as did a number of other small companies. Because of the worldwide recession, work was reduced in the main Welsh Steelworks, which also meant that most of the smaller providers would have to close.

Works manager, John Owens, thought that Dowlais Steel Works would stay open if it could stay profit making and increase product. It would then make sense not to be closed.

Sadly, John Owens was dreaming. Maggie Thatcher's Tory

government was in power and the fact that Merthyr was totally Labour wasn't going to help. The MP for Merthyr, Ted Rowlands, probably did his bit of shouting in the House of Commons, but he may as well have banged his head against a brick wall.

Looking back over my twenty-five years at Dowlais Steel Works, I reflect on the changes that had occurred. It had become good, well-paid employment for us all, and manager John Owen had given many a lift up the ladder. The last few years at the Works hold sad memories for me as I witnessed the death throes of what had once been a mighty steel works.

Not many realised the devastating effect the eventual closure of Dowlais Steel Works would have on the local community.

Workmen lost the security of having a regular wage paid into the bank and those that chose self-employment discovered probably for the first time the uncertainty of earning money that way. Many redundant employees had to settle for life on the pittance of dole money, while still having to cope with the pressures of paying the mortgage, petrol for the car, clothes for the children, etc. A lot of men had to share the full time company of their wives and family for the first time. Being unable to cope with the sudden changes caused health problems and many families split up.

Chapter 28

Goodbye Guest Keen and into Pub

After twenty-five years employed at Dowlais Steel Works, cushioned in the comfort of a massive industry that paid well for doing the minimum of work, I felt trapped and wanting the freedom of working for myself, and make the money that could reputedly be earned. Was I an optimist? Was I a fool? Probably both. Whichever, I took the bait and asked for redundancy. Goodbye Ivor Works. Thank you for twenty-five years of experience.

I was approached by a local builder to become his partner. Easy money, or so I thought. But, due to the mass redundancies in the valleys, the fastest growing business was the building trade. Unfortunately, due to the huge numbers of unskilled builders, the 'cowboy builder' flourished. I soon discovered also that some of the biggest villains were the long established building firms who used their knowledge to rip off clients and their skills to hide their cheating. Ah well, I'd already met crooks and villains in the steel industry and in the world of boxing. I'd met crooks involved in wholesale and retail grocery, confectionary and the clothing trade and now I was introduced to dodgy builders', dodgy builders merchants, dodgy householders, dodgy estate agents, dodgy accountants, dodgy solicitors and dodgy councillors. Boy oh boy it went on and on.

There were four of us in the firm and what a rum lot we were.

Then, April 1983, Hilary and I took over the Richards Arms Public House, Abercanaid, but we continued to live in the family home. The pub was situated in the centre of a row of terraced houses. As you entered the passageway, the bar was on the right, and on the left was a smoke room. To the rear, on the left was the singing room and on the right a small room with women's toilets behind that. The upper floor was a self contained flat.

I, in particular, was on cloud nine. Oh, what a marvellous life I was going to have flitting around the building sites all day, nipping in and out of the pub to socialise, visiting my gym in the evenings and travelling to boxing shows. It seemed all right to me. What a plonker I was! If only we'd known what was ahead of us!

We'd been in pubs aplenty and we'd been drunk aplenty, but like many others who dream of owning a village pub, we hadn't realised how demanding and stressful it could be. What we didn't know beforehand was that publicans have a short lifespan because of the stress and working in an unhealthy environment. Many became bankrupt, many were divorced, and alcoholism was an occupational hazard.

The Richards Arms became one of the busiest pubs in Merthyr. It was busy on Saturday night, busy on Sunday night and busy on Monday night. In fact, it was busy every night. From opening time to stop tap, and longer, the staff, Hilary and I pulled pints and halves, served shorts, poured bottles, cleaned tables and emptied ash trays. We told jokes and listened to jokes, and laughed at the jokes that weren't funny. We had to listen to men whose wives didn't understand them and offer comfort to those who said they felt ill and believed getting legless would make them feel better. We gave sympathy to those who explained they couldn't afford to redecorate their homes, but did not remind them that that was because they spent every night drinking in the pub. I began to get fed up and asked myself if all this was supposed to be socialising? I also forgot to mention, there was the daily cleaning up of the pub that included the vomit; there was the abuse and the fights and drunks. Aye, 'ang on. This wasn't just hard work, it was a constant treadmill, day and night, seven days a week and on top of my other businesses.

Six months later, tired out and depressed, we regretted having taken over the Richards Arms. We were tired of working the demanding hours and fed up of the socialising. We were fed up of listening to the same old jokes, fed up of customers treating the bar staff as if they were second class citizens there to be picked on, fed up of bending an ear, fed up of bloody-well pulling pints and yes, fed up of using matchsticks to hold my eyelids up while counting the money before going to bed. Hilary and I held an emergency conference and reluctantly agreed that since we were already in the pub trade and had committed ourselves we should now make a go of it. So, shit or bust, seven years and then we'd pack it in.

In the smoke room, a group of old codgers would spend their afternoons and most evenings putting the world to rights. Now, I have no disrespect for elderly gentlemen, but in the past the trend was for the men in the smoke room to use a spittoon. I'm not saying that they spat their phlegm straight into the bin, after all this was the twentieth century. They did spit their phlegm into a tissue first but why didn't they take the tissues to the toilet and flush them? I could never understand. Did they follow these habits at home, I wonder? Did they hell! Anyway, I didn't feel like cleaning out the spittoons so they had to go. For decades the gang of elders had not only drank in the smoke room but also held their meetings there. Dai kept telling me, 'Don't forget George, your regulars are your bread and butter,' as he stamped out his cigarette butt on the carpet with the heel of his shoe. I realised that controlling that little lot was going to be difficult.

Despite the disadvantages of having a pub, it wasn't all

doom and gloom because there were other things that gave us joy. Deborah and Julie decided to get married within six months of each other and walking down the aisle with my daughters on my arm was one of the proudest moments of my life. Julie and her husband, Robert Harries, provided Hilary and me with grand-daughter, Lisa, while Deborah and her husband, Robert Davies presented us with Luke, Jordan and Larah. Four lovely grandchildren who are the light of our lives.

The year was 1987 and despite working my socks off in the pub I still had boxing to think about. I arranged a match for one of my six-round fighters at a Sporting Club Show in Glasgow. I knew from experience how much of a drag it was to travel to Scotland, but my fighter had asked me to get him a nice earner and that was what had come up. The match was good and the money tidy but it was odds on that the Scottish lad would get a hometown decision if the fight was close. So here we go again, get to bed by one o'clock, snatch three hours sleep, wake up in a stupor and then drive bleary eyed to Troedyrhiw for Joe, call for my boxer and leave Merthyr at five in the morning to reach Glasgow in time for the boxer to rest before fighting. He couldn't afford to take a couple of days off work and so, with Joe sharing the driving, we travelled on the day of the fight and then drove back home to Merthyr straight after the fight. It was eight, long, tiring hours from Merthyr, along the motorway north into Scotland.

The Scots always gave us a good welcome, but when the bell sounded there was no love lost in the ring. It was a good even fight but, true to tradition, the Scots guy got the verdict. Still, I kept the opponent in mind. Another time, a different place and it would make a good return match. After the contest we had to face the drive back home and that was even more tiring than the journey up North.

Joe and I regularly swapped driving but there were narrow escapes. At one stage during the journey, Joe was driving, I was in the passenger seat and the boxer was asleep on the back seat.

As we drove along the dual carriageway between the M50 and Monmouth, I glanced at Joe who looked all right, then at the speedo which read eighty miles per hour. We were fast approaching a roundabout and I thought it funny that Joe hadn't started to slow down. A couple of hundred yards from the roundabout, I realised he'd had a lapse of concentration and shouted at him. Joe came to life and slammed the brakes on, the car turned sideways, slid towards the roundabout and was just about to crash when Joe took his foot off the brake and the car ran past the roundabout. What a narrow escape.

We arrived in Merthyr at about five o'clock in the morning. I took the fighter home before dropping Joe off at Troedyrhiw. Finally, on arriving home myself I think I could be forgiven for wishing I hadn't bothered. All that effort to take a six round boxer who would never achieve any better, and who would never provide me with an earner. After I had paid Joe, I was left out of pocket. But that was what boxing was all about.

Three hours later I'd hear the alarm and force my eyelids apart. Looking around the bedroom I realised that I was back in my own home. It was now time to knuckle down to pub business and clean after the cleaner, sort out the beer and open up at eleven o'clock. I'd climb out of bed, get dressed, get washed (maybe) and have a cup of tea before leaving for the pub. It wasn't until I'd walked the five hundred odd yards to the Richards Arms that I'd be fully awake. It's no wonder that many publicans reach for the whisky bottle for a livener in the morning, or at other times for that matter. I'd set the business in motion and the first to arrive would usually be former Merthyr Town footballer Trevor, waiting for a livener.

'Morning Trev, how's it going, butt?'

'Alright George, give me a minute, 'ad 'ard night last night, too much to drink.'

Trevor, small of stature and always neatly dressed would sit near the door waiting to see the next customer arrive. This would usually be Glan, who'd also had a hard night's drinking the previous night. He would come into the pub and saunter up to the bar and I'd greet the second customer of the day. 'Hello Glan, how are you this morning?'

Glan, who was also small, tidily dressed and along with Trevor could be considered a hardened drinker would roll his eyes, 'Give us a bottle, George, I'll tell you after.' And he'd sit next to Trevor who would interrupt by saying something like, 'It's up to the individual George,' hoping to start an argument. I'd walk away and leave them to it.

After a long week, Saturday night would arrive and many customers would sit in the back room listening to resident pianist Cyril (Poona) playing the piano like Les Dawson. But as the age of the piano disappeared from pubs the piano players were disappearing too. Glan's singing and Poona in accompaniment succeeded in keeping the customers away.

After two years of us being in the pub it was completely renovated, enabling Hilary to employ her cooking skills which attracted custom from all over South Wales. The sale of food, together with the sale of beer provided us with a good living, but it still wasn't an easy living by any means and there were also the rogues of the trade to deal with.

'Did I want to buy cheap beefburgers?'

'No thanks, you've nicked them from Abercanaid School.'

Next, a scruffy looking bloke would come into the pub, saunter up to the bar and whisper, 'Do me a favour George, let me book until my giro comes in next Tuesday?'

'Sorry, butt, I don't give beer on tick.'

The bar begins to fill with customers and a smartly dressed bloke enters followed by three other blokes.

'Right lads,' said the first bloke. 'What are you having to drink?' and leaning on the bar, he winked at me and said, 'And one for you landlord.' I refused.

A round of drinks and some bar meals were ordered and the flash guy pulled a chequebook out of his pocket. 'How much do that lot come to landlord?'

I asked him for his cheque guarantee card.

'I haven't got it with me,' he smirked. 'Don't worry my cheques don't bounce.'

Then, flash guy took the cheque off me and said, 'Look I know my card number,' and he wrote a number on the back of the cheque.

I shook my head. 'Sorry, butt, that's no good to me. If you haven't got your guarantee card you can't pay by cheque.'

He caught hold of my arm. 'Look landlord.'

But before he could continue I leant towards him, 'Look sunshine, if you haven't got a card give me the cash and no arguments.'

Flash guy then put his hand in his pocket, pulled out a handful of notes and paid what he owed.

I did get tucked up many times, but there you are, that's what comes from being too trusting. All sorts of tricks were tried on me to borrow money, or have beer on tick but I become hardened to it. Of course, there were always the bums and troublemakers but all in all there weren't too many of those.

Although I was busy in the pub I must have become addicted to work because I began planning to promote boxing shows. To ease my burden in the gym, friend and forever sparring partner, Graham Miles became trainer to my fighters, giving me time to conduct other business.

My boxer, Paul Boyce, having trouble with his hands retired from fighting but wanted to stay in boxing. We'd been pals for many years and jointly signed two Port Talbot boxers, welterweight Andy Morgan and flyweight Davy Jones. We also began promoting boxing shows together and our first show was at the Patti Pavilion, Swansea, where we had arranged for Davy Jones to fight West Walian Phil Dicks for the vacant Welsh Flyweight Championship.

It was our first boxing promotion together and we were keen to impress, paying attention to every detail. The main bout was arranged and the Boxing Board of Control informed. We hired

Paddy Burns as matchmaker to fix the rest of the bill. I arranged the printing and distribution of tickets and posters, organise security and a doctor, hire and check a weighing scale, and the numerous other jobs required to run a boxing show.

Baker Hire of Merthyr sponsored the show and manager, Jon Lee, worked hard with publicity and ticket selling. A Swansea boxing manager offered us the hire of his boxing ring and we arranged to collect and assemble it on the afternoon of the show.

The day of the show arrived and the 1pm weigh-in was attended by the boxers and their managers, Boxing Board Reps, a doctor, the press and television. The boxers who weighed in were medically examined by the doctor and everything went along smoothly.

In the afternoon Paul hired a lorry and we collected the ring and took it to the Patti Pavilion. When we started to assemble it, we discovered that a great deal of the ring was missing. Bolts had been lost, staging broken and ropes missing. What a mess and it was too late then to find another boxing ring to replace it. Paul managed to get hold of some bolts to replace the missing ones. We tied the broken ropes together and nailed wooden staging beneath the ring structure. We stood back to inspect our endeavors and started to breath easy. The show was ready to roll.

The evening arrived and the hall began to fill as attendants showed spectators to their seats. Businessmen sitting at ringside kept standing up pretending to look for someone but really, all they wanted was to let others know that they were in the best seats. Ex-boxers paraded around looking to renew old acquaintances. They were not concerned about where they sat, but were just happy to be in the world of boxing again.

Meanwhile the hall filled up and the first couple of fights went ahead and everything was fine. The top of the bill was introduced with Port Talbot's Davy Jones and West Walian Phil Dicks contesting for the vacant Welsh Flyweight Championship. The hall became quiet as the bell rang to start the first round and both fighters tore into each other. It was a war between two small men.

A couple of rounds had gone by when I suddenly noticed that the floor of the boxing ring was slowly moving. Then, I realized, with horror, that the ring was starting to collapse. Boxing Board official Cliff Curvis, who had also seen the floor movement ran around the ring, knelt by my side and said, 'George, the ring is collapsing! You've got to do something.' We both looked at the floorboards again and sure enough, as both boys banged away at each other the floor was slowly sinking.

Cliff Curvis had seen enough. 'I'll have to stop the contest,' he said.

Oh my God! If the fight was stopped there would be pandemonium. We'd have to give all the spectators a refund, the television wouldn't pay us, and the Welsh Championship would be declared void. What a tragedy.

'Hang on, Cliff. We'll fix it straight away,' I pleaded with him. He still looked doubtful but returned to his seat.

I tapped Paul on the shoulder. He'd been so interested in watching the fighters that he hadn't noticed the floorboards collapsing. 'Something's got to be done or Cliff will stop the fight,' I whispered, not wanting anyone else to hear. Paul called Phil, our Mr Fixit, who collected pieces of timber and disappeared beneath the ring. Cliff Curvis, ducking low so as not to block anyone's view, once again made his way to where I was standing besides the ring. 'It's got to be stopped, George,' he said, 'We can't let it go on any longer.'

We both looked at the flooring that was sinking lower and lower. 'Two minutes Cliff,' I pleaded, 'Just give us two minutes and it'll be fixed.' I didn't know how it was going to be fixed, I was just hoping.

After what seemed like an age the flooring stopped sinking and Phil emerged, smiling, from under the ring. All was A Okay.

The two flyweights battled away at each other for ten rounds in a tremendous contest that our man, Davy Jones, deservedly won.

Chapter 29

Epilogue

It was April 1990. The seven years that Hilary and I had agreed to stay in the pub were up and it was time to move on. The building firm, I'd already packed in. Getting work for my fighters became more of a concern than a pleasure, and travelling around the country to boxing shows was becoming a bind.

As I reflected on my past life, I accepted that marrying at a young age and having to rear a family on small wages gave me the incentive to achieve more and helped to mould me into what I became. But there were also many other influences including my early schooling at Caedraw and on to surviving the boring routine of Queen's Road Secondary Modern School. There was also my employment at Guest Keen Iron and Steel Works, Dowlais where I spent most of my working life.

Hilary and I became shopkeepers and publicans and I ventured into being a property developer and financier. But it was boxing that occupied a great part of my life and helped to provide a little extra for my family and give me some worldly knowledge.

I thought back to when I was eight years old and was introduced to boxing at the old Angel Hotel, and shortly after that when my father started a boxing gym in the Drill Hall,

Georgetown, in the 1950's. He reintroduced amateur boxing to Merthyr Tydfil, and discovered one of Wales's most famous boxers in the form of Howard Winstone. In doing so he triggered an era of boxing when boys achieved fame in both amateur and professional boxing and, once again, Merthyr Tydfil became a boxing town.

I look back at a past era in boxing that vanished, like the recognized landmarks which signified the old traditions of Welsh boxing. The first boxing gym in my memory disappeared with the demolition of the old Angel Buildings in Merthyr. The former Billiards Hall in Penydarren, famous as Eddie Thomas's gym where world champions trained, also fell to the demolition gang. In Troedyrhiw, the former infants school that became my boxing gym was part of the council's clearance scheme. And with the school went the cast iron fire grate and the ghosts of old fighters spinning their yarns. Cramped, inadequate, boxing gyms with the smell of 'boxing' that seemed to have a magic formula for making good fighters, vanished. With the advent of television, the majority of small hall boxing shows disappeared and with them the many journeymen fighters who had been prepared to travel the country looking for small hall work.

I now look at my hands, crippled from a lifetime of punching and my swollen eyebrows creased with scar tissue from cuts received in the boxing ring. I feel constant pain in my arthritic body and think back to the old fighters crowded around the blazing coal fire in my gym. But, do I regret becoming a boxer or taking part in a brutal sport? No, I do not. A lifetime in the world of boxing has provided me with much of substance and many pleasures. Boxing is a dangerous sport, but no more dangerous than many other sports. People become professional boxers for the thrill of participation, the atmosphere and excitement, the glory and the money.

Once, there was a need to fight for survival but then, eventually, fighting became a sport. Men will always fight each other and for many reasons. Controlled boxing must therefore be allowed to continue, otherwise men will once again resort to fighting on the mountainside.